Richard Randolph

Windfalls

Richard Randolph

Windfalls

ISBN/EAN: 9783744652070

Printed in Europe, USA, Canada, Australia, Japan

Cover: Foto ©Thomas Meinert / pixelio.de

More available books at **www.hansebooks.com**

BY THE AUTHOR OF

"ASPECTS OF HUMANITY."

[REVISED EDITION.]

PHILADELPHIA:

HENRY LONGSTRETH,

740 SANSOM STREET.

1889.

WINDFALLS.

"CHARITY NEVER FAILETH."

Man's wisdom takes its rise in fear;
And "fear hath torment," though in hearts sincere.
God's wisdom flows in perfect LOVE,
And lifts the fallen soul all fear above.

Be ours to search that flood of strength,
To trace its rise and prosecute its length,
And view its breadth, as finite man
Such boundless bliss may incompletely scan.

See first a righteous fear induce
Faith in a guidance from which sin broke loose,—
Enlightened faith, as taught by grief
Unknown before its act of unbelief.

From faith so warned to keep its course,
And persevering, grows a nobler force,—
A faith renewed, with larger scope,
In which fear falls, and is replaced by hope.

So stayed by hope and turned toward things
Not seen, for else hope were not hope, faith brings
The faithful soul into such state,
That all its works on LOVE and knowledge wait.

Then faith and hope, not slain like fear,
Are lost, in that they can no more appear.
Through doubt and shame their fires endure;
LOVE is not LOVE, except its flame be pure.

So man, in vision clear, discerns
How all GOD'S universe uninjured burns,
As burned the bush which MOSES saw,
And yields his heart to LOVE'S eternal law.

CONTENTS.

1*

WINDFALLS.

A SALUTATION.

Greet ye one another with an holy kiss."—1 Cor. xvi. 20, ETC.

GOD speed thee, struggling neighbor !
  All blessings on thy head !
May we be one in labor,
  Till to temptation dead !

So shall we stand united ;
  While parted, both might fall,
Although of God invited,
  Who would be all in all.

He is before all creatures ;
  In Him we all consist,
And glorify his features,
  Or foul them, as we list.

We tread the world of matter
  By means of outward sense,
Whose visions often flatter,
  While veiling violence.

But as we win the graces
  Which wait upon his will,
We read in fellow-faces
  The signs of good and ill.

And if we be connected
   On the internal ground,
With joy are we affected
   When outward links are found.

With honest purpose meeting,
   All doubting we dismiss ;
Count every word a greeting,
   And every work a kiss.

MATHEMATICS TYPICAL OF
UNIVERSAL SCIENCE.

———

"Mathematics is only common elementary philosophy, and philosophy is only higher mathematics."—NOVALIS.

[A WORD OF CAUTION.—Be entreated, gentle reader! before devoting time and attention to an appreciation of the ensuing disquisition, to pause and reflect upon the difference between a true assurance and a false. The true explorer and reporter of the realms of thought, relying wholly for fortune and favor on the consciousness that the Truth is inherently larger and clearer as well as fairer than any demonstration of it which he can hope to give, pretends not to foresee the suggestions which his report shall awaken in any minds. But while he is thus secured from the temptation to work for mere sensational effect, there must always be effects which he can imagine might be produced in any hearer or reader. He may be a true author, while a very partial seer. The mere literary pretender, however, goes a step farther in the blindness of his faith, assuming that he may be generally as well as particularly unconscious of any virtue passing through him. As the author of NIGHT THOUGHTS has freely delineated him in one of his epistles to the author of THE DUNCIAD,

> "Perhaps a title has his fancy smit;
> Or a quaint motto, which he thinks has wit.
> He writes, in inspiration puts his trust.
> Tho' wrong his thoughts, the gods will make them just.
> Genius directly from the gods descends,
> And who by labor would distrust his friends?
> . Thus having reasoned with consummate skill,
> In immortality he dips his quill;
> And, since blank paper is denied the press,
> He mingles the whole alphabet by guess,
> In various sets, which various words compose,
> Of which he hopes mankind the meaning knows."

Prudent reader! if thy time and attention shall here be devoted in vain, cast not all the blame on him who thus forewarns thee. If unaccustomed or averse to "thinking about thinking," examine first the next presented and shorter article on NUMBER, which may possibly furnish a fit introduction to this, probably a more than sufficient substitute for it.]

TRUTH, in one of its aspects, may be defined to be the power of coalescence. The observation is doubtless as old as Humanity, with distinctness proportioned to the saga-

The unity of truth.

city of the observer, and must ever continue with increasing clearness to stimulate and to reward the zeal of Nature's hopeful explorers, that the bound-ary lines of her provinces, as they are fondly and unavoidably called, have in Nature no actual existence. The distinctions of diverse Science, originating exclusively although uncon-sciously in the realm of imagination, as ideas of more or less temporary value, are not natural, but artificial. In technical parlance, they exist, while they exist, not objectively, or in fact, but subjectively only, or in our partial modes of percep-tion and of thought. They are all doomed more or less grad-ually to vanish, as the domain of intellect shall be extended. Whether we will receive it or whether we will forbear, there is a progressive revelation of Nature, in which coalition and co-operation everywhere announce the omnipresent Deity. All things run together, although their wondrous fusion may be duly realized only in the full radiance of that celestial Light, whose straggling emanations even are wont to dazzle our mortal gaze into temporary blindness.

This doctrine of a pervading unity in Na-

Essential to intelli-gence and certainty.

ture, like every other principle of truth, may be said to be an intuitive perception of the healthy human soul. Like others it may be overlain and concealed in the very abundance of fragmentary attainment, and so become temporarily an unavailable if not superfluous element of wisdom. Perhaps even more than others has this doctrine suffered this fate in latter ages. But such fate cannot be final. The lost link must from time to time re-appear in the inevitable successions of universal thought. The forgotten or neglected stone must still retain its place in

the eternal arch of truth. How many a weary soul may be
even now looking wistfully back from the distraction of the
"much learning" under which the modern mind has been
staggering onward, to those clear morning hours of philosophy,
to the ages at once of poverty and of promise, when the
pristine freshness of intellect had as yet in no wise yielded to
a sophisticated insensibility ; but when the Pythagorases and
the Platos could stride freely over the whole domain of knowledge, and demand, nothing doubting, from every fact of
every kind its contribution to the universal scheme! A lame
induction had not then led mankind into the persuasion that
there were two sorts of truth in the world ; the one of which
was certain, and the other at best but probable. Philosophers
then, little dreaming that the truly provable (*probabile*)
could be supposed to differ from the truly experimental,
seem to have been not only willing but anxious to make
themselves extreme upon all points of belief, as if conscious
that in such trustful daring lay the most coercive conservat-
ism,—the surest preventive of actual extravagance in whatever direction. Their faith in the every-day details of knowledge did not, upon the occurrence of apparent discrepancies
therein, extinguish their faith in the underlying principles
which maintain an ever-increasing predominance in truly
reflecting minds, nor yet in the ever-unfolding and possibly
unbroken consistency of the whole course of the created
universe. Intellectual prosperity has now too largely relaxed
our intellectual rigor. Man, being " in honor," " understandeth not." The very success of those hardy ancients in their
introvertive industry has come to be regarded as failure, and
their strength as little more than weakness. How have we
been almost taught even to " account their lives madness, and
their end without honor !" Nevertheless, how well might we
long for an adequate share of the same method and coherency
of intelligence which they so triumphantly derived from their
scanty materials, and without which our mental wealth must
be an incumbrance, and may become a bane.

Certainty to be
despaired of in
no department of
kuowledge.
It is universally acknowledged that certainty
is pre-eminently attainable in the science of
Mathematics. It may therefore be assumed
that if the foundations of knowledge are in any
case accessible by all men, they must be especially so in the
principles of that science. It is the aim of this essay to show
that there is a universal thought which is the object of individual thinking, or that all science is based upon pure observation, with no empirical admixture of hypothetical, or theoretical anticipation of natural facts, on the part of the observing
mind. If this can be demonstrated as a primary theorem even
in Mathematics, not only must every vestige and avenue of
uncertainty be excluded from that science, but by virtue of the
applicability of the same laws of perception and of thought
which have there such free and fruitful scope, to the development of other branches of knowledge which are undisputedly
grounded upon the same universal principle of direct observation or rigid inference, the objective reality of all, in foundation and in superstructure, must be equally established. The
whole creation will thus be intelligibly presented to our imagination as a continuous temple of truth and beauty, albeit
more or less vaguely, while the lingering veil of moral evil
shall at all obscure the perfect designs of the divine Creator,
and retard the full appreciation of the willing worshiper.

Mathematics a
type of all know-
ledge in its Origin,
Development and
Tradition. Theses
propounded.
Taking Mathematics, then, as a type of Science at large, let us proceed to consider its
history under the three heads expressed in the
three following Theses; viz:

I. That the science of Mathematics, like
other provinces of knowledge, originates exclusively in the
observation of certain objective qualities of things.

II. That its cultivation is conducted only by the same intellectual processes of imaginary analysis and imaginary combination, otherwise called Abstraction and Reasoning, which
are adopted in other sciences; and not by the aid of any sys-

tem or prelude of mere hypothesis, apart from those processes or unknown to other sciences.

III. That its exposition, or communication from mind to mind, being accomplished by the emblematic embodying of the ideas and subjective processes thus arising in appropriate objective symbols, which symbols have not the same immediate connection and apparent identity with their subjects, which the original objects had with their proper images or perceptions in the mind,* depends upon and proves (as does the language of all original thought) the existence, assumed and admitted though not expressed, of a like reflective capacity in each of the parties, and also of a will on either side struggling for the union of agreement. In other words, the essential elements and methods of all speech are involved in even the simplest mathematical demonstrations.

In approaching the examination of these Theses, it becomes a preliminary duty to assume some definition of the subject which they concern, with whatever novelty of form present perspicuity may require. Let us then simply define Mathematics to be the science which treats of Matter, as it is known in its universal properties, whether original or derived. *For the definition of Mathematics,*

The consideration of this definition of course involves a still preliminary decision as to what are the universal properties of matter which are objects of knowledge, with some inquiry by the way into the nature and objects of sensation in general. *some analysis necessary of the properties of matter, or the relations of matter to sense.*

* It is impossible but that any one who does not thus distinguish between the connection of words with thoughts and that of thoughts with things, will be often disappointed in his attempts at conversation or demonstration. The more artificial and superficial connection between words and thoughts is so apt to supersede and render nugatory the more natural and profound connection of thoughts with things, that there can be no profitable communion between parties neither of whose memory is in this respect rectified by philosophy, or by the religious faith which includes the power of philosophy.

In the present state of general science, it
cannot be presumed that all the properties
which may be ascribed to matter, are strictly
peculiar to it. Impenetrability, for instance, may be supposed to be equally a property of the universal medium,
sometimes called " ether," or more definitely *passimede,* *
which interpenetrates and connects the atoms and massive
aggregations which are properly known as matter. By this
attribute of impenetrability, this refined medium may perhaps more immediately affect the nobler organs of " special "
sense, those, namely, of sight, smell, taste and hearing (of
this at least as regards the direction of sound), without that
intervening mechanical impression which seems necessary to
the action of the " general " senses known as the tactile and
the muscular. But inasmuch as these baser senses may be
found to suffice of themselves for the apprehension of the
attributes of matter, and the use of those finer in the appreciation of matter by these attributes or qualities, is merely
the result of an education which they receive by their co-
operation with the baser, it seems incumbent upon us to
confine our attention to the senses of Touch and of Muscular
Resistance, as the primary and proper avenues of all mathematical ideas, so far as those ideas may be found to be derived from without us.

Transcendental matter. (margin note)

The inherent properties of matter, or objects of "general" sensation, may be thus
enumerated :

Proximate analysis of the properties of matter, pure and mixed. (margin note)

(1.) *Impenetrability;* or distinctness of substance, by means of which the presence of one sort of matter
excludes that of any other sort, or of any other portion of the
same sort.

(2.) *Interrupted extent;* or finity of substance, whereby
matter is susceptible of every variety of form.

(3.) *Duration;* or permanence of existence, which is also,

---

* From *passim, medium.* A mere suggestion by the author.

or at least may be, interrupted or limited, so far as it is an object of sense.

(4.) *Inertia;* or dependence of condition, exhibited alike in the phenomenon of motion and in that of rest.

(5.) *Impressibility;* or mutability of condition, exhibited under the influence of chemical or other invisible power, by the variations of motion in all forms of attraction and repulsion.

Those chemical or physiological habitudes of matter which are distinct from these mechanical, such as Temperature, Color, Taste, etc., though observable, some or all of them, *Some mixed properties not universal, and so not concerned in Mathematics.* in combination with all matter, appear not to belong inherently to matter itself, but to be plainly imparted to it by the immaterial agency or agencies concerned, which cannot as yet be accurately designated, even by name. Again, the universal qualities of matter just now recounted, are probably not all in themselves primary and elementary. But that question is here irrelevant, since they have yet to be combined among themselves to furnish the perceptions and ideas which are the primary and secondary materials of mathematical science.

These combinations, or compound and still universal qualities of matter, as known in the mind, may be thus announced : *Composition of mathematical materials, present and represented.*

First; the perception or idea of Space, resulting from (1) in combination with (2).

Second; the perception or idea of Multiplicity or Number, from simultaneous repetitions of the same combination.

Third; the idea of Time from (1) and (3),with the aid of memory. The idea of Number may also thus arise, by the same aid ; and by this duality of origin, the idea of Number may become a representative of both Space and Time in conjunction with their subordinate attribute of quantitative proportion. And it is here worthy of note, that since Time differs from Space in being known only through the aid of memory, its idea can never, like that of Space, be supposed to be instantaneously present in our calculations. Therefore, although we deal with Space, as an idea, either immediately or through the representation of Number, we can only estimate and apply the idea of Time, by the imaginary or representative means.

Fourth; the perception or idea of Motion or Velocity, from (1) and (4), under the influence of the unknown power or powers which we can only vaguely designate by the terms vital, chemical, cosmical, etc.

Fifth; the perception or idea of Force or Momentum, from (1) and (5), also under the influence of power acting from beyond the sphere of natural perception.

We already find a corroboration of our assumed definition of Mathematics, in the observation that these last-named cognitions, though not, like that of Time, dependent in any degree upon previous mental evidence, can, like it, only enter into mathematical inquiries by the representation of Space or Number; the reason in both cases being essentially the same, namely, that a part of the evidence upon which they arise is simply foreign to matter, as matter.

The assumed definition incidentally corroborated.

In accordance with this enumeration of its proximately elementary materials, we may now repeat in fuller form our previously assumed definition of Mathematics, as being the science which treats of Matter, as known in its universal and inherent but compound properties or qualities, Space, Number, and (so far as its nature appears) Time, and in the partly inherent and partly derived compound properties or qualities, Motion and Force. We thus also, it must be remarked, arrive at a re-statement * of the first of our three

Its farther consideration merged in that of the first " Thesis."

---

* Although this Essay in its original shape was written before the appearance of DR. WHEWELL'S *Novum Organon Renovatum*, it is with some mortification that I confess my ignorance of that work until this had been revised on the eve of publication. With the exception of the brief mention made of In-

Theses in more explicit form, except inasmuch as the actual origin of every science consists in the application of observing powers to the observable things. Let us now repeat and examine those Theses in detail.

I. "That the science of Mathematics, like other provinces of knowledge, originates exclusively in the observation of certain objective qualities of things."

This first Thesis being, as just now remarked, little more than a repetition of the assumed definition of the science, particular consideration of it may now be limited to an examination of such objections against the new definition, as may probably arise from a comparison with old ones. These may be considered under two heads :

Possible objections to it anticipated.

1. The subjects of Infinity and Nihility, which although out of the reach of human observation may perhaps by some be inad-

Its omissions, only apparent.

duction and Deduction in the text on p. 25, I am constrained to throw into the margin any remarks suggested by and extracts derived from that lucid and compendious code of progressive Philosophy. The citation next following may possibly assist the reader to bear in mind the distinction assumed in the text above, between the definition of the province, and the beginning of the work of Mathematics,—between the verbal designation of the field, and the actual breaking of the ground :—" In collecting scientific truths by Induction we often find a Definition and a Proposition established at the same time,—introduced together, and mutually dependent on each other. The combination of the two constitutes the inductive act, and we may consider the Definition as representing the superinduced Conception, and the Proposition as exhibiting the Colligation of Facts." (Bk. 2, Ch. 5, § 5.)

Here, as well as anywhere may also be cited some remarks which may perhaps to some minds enforce the external origin of our ideas of Number, Space, etc., by showing that forgetfulness of that origin is, or would be, only natural ; so that our primitive perceptions must be more or less laboriously mined out, so to speak, from present accumulations of knowledge, however comparatively vast or meagre : " In every inference by Induction, there is a Conception superinduced upon the Facts." (Bk. 2, Ch. 5, § 3.) " Although in every Induction a new Conception is superinduced upon the Facts, yet this once effectually done, the novelty of the Conception is overlooked, and the Conception is considered as a part of the Fact." (Bk. 2, Ch. 6, § 3.) See also Bk. 3, Ch. 4, § 4.

vertently supposed to lie within the range of mathematical inquiry, are not necessarily, and therefore not scientifically to be so regarded. It is indeed often necessary to advert to them ; but they may then be more simply regarded as forming the unavoidable boundaries, than as contributing to the subject materials of the science.

Its innovations, essential. 2. It is scarcely necessary to remark that widely different views have prevailed from those now presented as to the nature and origin of our ideas of Space, Time, and Number ; and as it is from this previous prevalence that exceptions to the present Thesis and definition are chiefly to be apprehended, a careful consideration of them becomes here expedient.

Space, being deemed capable of existing in the form of surface without bulk or capacity, and in that of linear extension without either surface or bulk, and being regarded as something which in itself partakes of infinitude, has thence been naturally supposed to have an existence, finitely in the human intelligence, infinitely in the divine, wholly independent of matter.* Time, also, probably in part from the circumstance of its requiring an obvious mental effort for its apprehension ; and partly, perhaps, from its being found the most important† of mundane resources,—the uniform channel of every external influence which maintains or modifies the condition of man,—has had a like independent and purely intellectual

---

* Probably the idea which is most generally conveyed by the current modes of defining and treating of Space, is that of a sort of ocean in which material things exist much as fish are scattered through the sea. And it may therefore perhaps at first sight appear as absurd to think of Space as being a quality of matter, as it would be to call the sea an attribute of fishes. But it must be noticed that the analogy fails in an essential particular. The fish displaces the sea, so that where one is, the other is not. Probably no sane person will assert the same of matter in Space.

† Possibly this peculiar importance of Time may be finally found to result from the fact of its not being universally a quality of matter except under the "curse" (Gen. iii. 17) which the earth incurred in consequence of the fall of Adam ; of which curse mutability, the universal measure of Time, may be an essential and representative feature.

or even spiritual existence ascribed to it. Numbers, we are
in the habit of using so freely in their imaginary or abstract
meaning, sometimes as a gymnastic labor, and sometimes
as a wholesome relaxation of the mind, that it may be still
less surprising that we should lose sight of their exterior
origin.

However these misapprehensions may have Mischiefs of tra-
arisen, it is easily to be understood how, in ditional confusion.
accordance with them, the science of Mathematics has happened to be defined in a mode very different from that here
suggested, that is, as being wholly subjective in its nature, or
originating solely in the mind.* That it is accordingly a structure based upon mere hypothesis, or upon assumed dogmata
for which no demonstrable authority could be adduced ;—that
its sure working and safe guidance are therefore merely a
lucky coincidence, and are no example or evidence of any
attainable principle of certainty in human affairs—any pre-
siding order or convincing unity of truth ;—but that, so far as
appears, all things are under the direction of a capricious
power of Fate, or mere law of Chance, which may tolerate
this inferior and partial uniformity (to such the solitary mystery of the universe, the eye of course, seeing in all things
"only what it brings with it the power to see") merely as
the tangible substratum which is requisite to uphold the
chaotic riot of a libertine life ;—these are the conclusions
which the ingenuity and influence of the votaries of vice have
not been slow to forge, and to link as inferences to that im-
movable staple of primary consciousness, which mathematical
truth in some way gives to all. Scholars, by confusing objective materials with subjective processes, have necessarily
curtailed the true import of the science in its spiritual as well

---

* The intellect of ages may be said to speak in these words of the eminent and excellent philosopher and historian of Science, already quoted :—
"The pure Mathematical Sciences can hardly be called Inductive Sciences.
Their principles are not obtained by Induction from Facts, but are necessarily assumed in reasoning upon the subject-matter which those Sciences involve."—*Nov. Org. Ren.*, B. 2, ch. 9.

as in its material aspect ; and the twofold mutilation can only
be apologized for as being in accordance with the treatment
received at their hands, perhaps inevitably under any heretofore prevailing *régime* of metaphysics,* by that coveted abstract and educt of all knowledge, which is termed the Science of Ontology.   For it is surely observable that earnest
and consecutive reasoners upon this comprehensive theme,
have been almost uniformly landed, according to their taste
and previous training, either in the extravagance of an empty
materialism on the one hand, or in that of an exclusive spirit-
ualism on the other : while those who have advocated more
catholic doctrine have as generally done so by a process rather
of compromise than of comprehension, having been either
secured, at the expense of consistency, by an original and insuperable dread of the glaring incompleteness ; or else influ-
enced, however indirectly, by the overwhelming weight of
the practical perceptions of the as yet unlearned mass of
mankind.   So little, it seems, may one science, or all science,
avail to prove that which in fact must be the very beginning
of any science, or learning, or proving, namely, that there are
present to the operation both an animating soul and an animated organism,—each with its congenial adjuncts.

                      Waiving, however, any actual appeal to
Its existence de-   metaphysical standards as a thing here un-
monstrable by ad-   called for, let us simply test by recognized
mitted axioms.   and rigid mathematical law, these speculative
views of the subjective nature of Space and Number, and of
Time so far as it can be represented by them in mathematical
investigation.

                      Any number of nothings results in Nothing,
First, as to Num-   as any fraction of Infinity remains infinite, for
ber.   the one reason above intimated, that those sub-

---

* In the words of a deservedly popular writer, "The establishment of a
philosophy of discovery and invention must await the establishment of a
philosophy of the mind which discovers and invents."—EDWIN P. WHIPPLE
on the Philosophy of BACON.

jects not being objects of perception, are unalterable even in idea, by the means of science. It is surely in vain to say in illustration of the subjective doctrine of Number, that "two and two make four," and that "the whole is greater than the part," and to argue as is usual, that these and other such phrases have an ideal or intelligible truth apart from any relation to numerable or measurable objects. For these expressions then must mean, that "two nothings and two nothings make four nothings," and that "the whole of nothing is greater than the part of nothing;" which are at best but random and gratuitous assertions, since by our acknowledged rule the two nothings and two nothings do not make four nothings, any more than they make one, or any other number of nothings: neither is the whole of nothing greater than the part of nothing, but by the same principle precisely equal to it. The subjective origin of the idea of Number thus exhibits itself as but an imaginary corner-stone of science.

The similar fiction of the "three dimensions" of Space, two at least of which can only exist subjectively, convenient, necessary, Secondly, as to Space. and even beautiful, as it may seem to be, may in like manner be regarded as unfounded and inexpedient. Space must have at least a differential* value in two directions, conjoined with an estimable value in the remaining one, to make it truly appreciable. In this case the appreciable dimension will be mere length, and we will have a substantial and measurable line. If it be appreciable in two directions, we have a surface or area which is also a tangible reality, and which is estimable by the measured line. If it be appreciable in the third direction also, we have again genuine Space, now rendered complete to the sense, and also

---

* That is, a value such as may always be imagined, which shall be definite in itself, and yet too small to be estimated in its results except by its practical equality with other like values on the one hand, or by its unaltered ratio to them when they have been reduced to the same degree, on the other.

estimable by the repeated application of the measured line.
We have thus an evidence for the objective nature of Space,
supplied by the mode in which alone it is conceivable for the
idea of Space to have originated. Again, both surface and
bulk being estimable by arithmetical multiplication, and
even length being always denotable by Number, we find a
confirmation of this view in our mode of computing Space,
which is identical with the argument already supplied by
the consideration of Number; the contrary view being here
also a violation of the inevitable law, that nothing produces
nothing. Two triangles having their three sides equal, each
to each, the lines and surfaces being defined in the old mode,
can thus be equal to each other, only as they are also equal
to a quadrangle containing two figures so defined, or to any
other such impossible polygon; that is, by being each equal
to nothing.

Extraneous In-
ducements to rec-
tification.

In quitting this branch of our subject, it may
not be superfluous to remark, that although
the views now advocated, must, as received,
occasion some slight modification in the language of Mathematics, this result cannot but be ultimately of
use, if it be only in the clearing of the gateways to the science
in its different departments, and so smoothing the paths of
beginners. Perhaps even minds familiarized to the prevailing
inaccurate modes of expression, may find the temporary dis-
location of ideas incurred in such a change amply compensated
by an expanding appreciation of the truth of the homespun
axiom, that "Well begun is half done," and by the wholesome assurance, that truth in general can only be thoroughly
appreciated in so far as the end may be seen in the beginning.

II. "That its cultivation is conducted only by the same intellectual processes of imaginary analysis and imaginary combination, otherwise called Abstraction and Reasoning, which
are adopted in other sciences; and not by the aid of any

system or prelude of mere hypothesis, apart from those processes, or unknown to other sciences."

The consideration of the second Thesis has
been in a great degree anticipated in that of Imaginative insight the clue of de-
the first. It has now been argued that mere velopment.
hypothesis does not either primarily furnish
the elementary facts of mathematical knowledge, nor mingle
permanently with the process of their intellectual apprehension and combination. It remains to be shown that the continued development of these facts and processes in an ever-
serviceable system, is also essentially free from arbitrary
assumption, and adheres to the basis of a true or original
ground in nature, notwithstanding that that ground may even
in this comparatively prosaic science, be somewhat concealed
and forgotten, in consequence of the specific materials which
are the subjects of systematic development, being often themselves a mental development or construction thereupon. This
imaginative mode of development, and seeming loss of the
foundation in the continuing superstructure, may perhaps be
most readily illustrated by an analysis and comparison of the
four primary operations of Arithmetic.

Two only of these operations, Addition and
Subtraction, can be said actually to occur in Examples.
nature, and to be truly imitated in our calculations, as any
simple idea in mind or memory imitates or reflects a perception of nature. Multiplication and Division cannot occur out
of the mind, except as it may be allowable so to speak of
them as imaginary consequences of repeated additions and
subtractions. Addition having occurred by the repetition in
nature of several equal or like elements, the quality of Number thus comes distinctly and impressively into view ; and
being, by the legitimate action of the imagination, abstracted
from the process of Addition as a ready representative of the
productive agent, this quality of Number has quite naturally
received first the imaginary office, and then the name, of
Multiplier. The mathematical process of Multiplication is

the retracing,* in a reverse order, of the growth which thus arises, as it were, from external nature into the mind. That is, as in the searching appreciation of the operation without us, we rise from the result therein observed, through an imaginary multiplication to an imaginary multiplier; so, when we proceed to anticipate by calculation the result of any like operation probably or possibly to occur in nature, we begin with realizing the " abstract" multiplier in the mind, pursue it downward through its mental combination or multiplication with the " concrete "† number concerned, and alight, with all confidence in the result, upon the common ground of concrete ideas, with an intelligence of natural truth as clear as if we were remembering facts as they had formerly happened, instead of predicting them from an exploration of their relations. The connection between Subtraction and Division is of course quite analogous to that between Addition and Multiplication. Addition and Subtraction are therefore distinguished as being simply ideal imitations in the mind, of what may have actually occurred externally, the ideal numbers not being severed from the concrete association in which they are received into the mind from without; in Multiplication and Division, if they are intelligently performed, man adopts a course of his own, whereby he estimates the slow results of material changes without waiting to see them or even to suppose them in detail. A true imaginative insight, an intelligence dwelling in the secret modes of his perceptions rather than in the obvious matter of them, is evidently necessary in the first place to discover to him the fact that the abstract conception of Number, when combined with the concrete in the way

---

* "Induction moves upward, and Deduction, downward, on the same scale."—WHEWELL, *Nov. Org. Ren.*, Bk. 2, ch. 6, § 18.

† The reader, if there shall be one, who may not at once recognize the justness of the distinction between the "abstract" and the "concrete" ideas of Number, as applied respectively to the multiplier and the multiplicand, is invited to an examination of the old arithmetical riddle,—to take first the square of twenty-five cents, and then the square of the quarter of a dollar, and reconcile the results, if he can.

of Multiplication and Division, must give the results, while avoiding the labor, of repeated Addition and Subtraction : and the same insight remains as his sufficient authority for classifying these processes rather according to their mental rank, as indicated by their comparative complexity and analytical history, than by a reference to the associations under which they occur or originate in nature. Thus, upon the common principles of natural science, Multiplication and Division become recognized as allied species constituting a true genus,—Addition and Subtraction in like manner forming a separate genus, of mathematical rules, derivable by processes of induction, and available for purposes of deduction.*

Our observations upon mathematical science thus far, concern its development, as distinguished from its demonstration, and are equally applicable to its four cardinal branches

Sources of the doctrine of hypothesis.

of Arithmetic, Geometry, Algebra, and Mechanics. In all of these the constructive work of imagination, inseparable from all development of Science, may assume the appearance of random hypothesis, as the form of hypothesis may be incident to the work of exposition. But to make hypothesis therefore the foundation or the law of any of them, were evidently to confound the channel with the stream. All science consisting in the interpretation of nature, and all truth being one, all permanent progress of the so-called special sciences must be the harmonious growth of component parts of a single whole. The fewness, simpleness and universality of the primary materials of Mathematics, by securing a facility of culture, have induced an overshadowing ideal development, in which their original relationship seems to have been entirely lost sight of. This remarkable obscuration is wholly

---

* "In *Induction*, besides a mere collection of particulars, there is always a *new conception*, or principle of connection and unity supplied by the mind, and superinduced upon the particulars. . . . In *deductive* reasonings, the general principles are assumed, and the question is concerning their application and combination in particular cases."—WHEWELL, *Nov. Org. Ren.*, B. 2, ch. 6.

traceable to the fact, that the foundation of the science in the sensible phenomena of nature being comparatively base as well as broad, the development of universal thought, in rising successively above the level of higher foundations, contributes comparatively more from itself in bulk to this meaner, even as it derives to itself comparatively more in quality, from those nobler sciences. In the eagerness of mental appetite, the influences of quantity and quality, of matter and spirit, have remained in some degree undistinguished, and the process of discovery been confounded with that of demonstration.

A few general observations upon the admissibility and necessity of hypothetical assumption in the work of demonstration now only remain to be adduced in confirmation of our third Thesis.

III. " That its exposition, or communication from mind to mind, being accomplished by the emblematic embodying of the ideas and subjective processes thus arising, in appropriate objective symbols, which symbols have not the same immediate connection and apparent identity with their subjects which the original objects had with their proper images or perceptions in the mind, depends upon and proves (as does the language of all original thought) the existence, assumed and admitted though not expressed, of a like reflective capacity in each of the parties, and also of a will on either side struggling for the union of agreement. In other words, the essential elements and methods of all speech are involved even in the simplest mathematical demonstrations."

Origin of language in a lower, and use in a higher, consciousness.

We must here remark the fact, which perhaps first found definite expression in the famous work * of JOHN HORNE TOOKE, and which can never long remain a mystery among thinking men, that all the materials of language have originated in man's experience of the external world, as derived either from surrounding things or from his own physical nature.

* " EPEA PTEROENTA ; or, The Diversions of Purley."

And mankind, it may be presumed, are now also prepared both to acknowledge and to understand the complementary fact, (through want of which the sagacity even of a Tooke was so much at fault,) that words, so derived, may be available as a medium or spiritual communication, in consequence (and only so) of some appreciable sameness or similarity between those perceptions of sensible objects with which the words originated, and the larger thoughts or deeper emotions which the same words are eventually used to express. The fact first named may be seen to result from the truth universally observed or observable, that mankind, whether or not they may ultimately attain to a method of mutual acquaintance and understanding apart from the avenues of sense, are at least by their inherited nature incapable of any intercourse except through those avenues, and by means which must be adapted to their restricted mode of transit. And in that complementary fact of the natural availability of such language for such elevated service, the sameness or similarity of meaning in spheres so diverse is equally accounted for, by that unity of experience under diversity of circumstances, which distinguishes manhood, upon the assumption (the general or parent hypothesis, which here becomes necessary simply because it is possible and remains as the only supposition which will account for the facts) that there is a pre-established analogy, or an identity of relations, between the material universe and the living body of man on the one hand, and a spiritual universe and the human soul on the other.

The equal reality of these two spheres of existence is therefore, in direct opposition to the inference or intimation of the author of *All figurative language, therefore, a form of hypothesis.* "WINGED WORDS," implied in the secret constitution of language, together with an acquired but enduring consciousness of a certain identity in their experimental significance;—an identity which may be occasional and temporary in its details, (owing to the variable and transitory nature of our merely physical impressions,) but which is sufficient to originate and

to reinforce indefinitely a language adequate to all social
purposes. Hence it is observable that words, while retaining
their primitive meaning, and even after losing it, if familiarized in any definite acceptation, are liable to be used in two
several modes: in their familiar meaning, either primitive or
secondary, they may be employed to indicate the familiar
idea of a thing or fact, upon the specific ground of a perception, present or past, being common to both parties; and
they may be appealed to in order to convey an analogical
meaning, the origin of which has now been conjecturally defined, on the before mentioned general ground of like reflective capacities and co-operating wills.

And, as such, of   This distinction, thus arrived at between the
but transitional or   two methods of language, the literal and the
educational value.   figurative, or the prosaic and the poetic, not
only indicates and explains that objectively neutral or ambig-
uous character of all language, by which the same utterance
may at some times and to some minds be poetical, which at
a subsequent time or to an already familiarized mind may be
simply prosaic; but suggests the farther observation that
poetry must take the lead of prose in all education,—in every
propagation, whether earlier or later, of actual thought. In
such a process mind must ever reach toward mind with
strictly hopeful or spiritual purpose; and the struggle becom-
ing effectual only through the common recognition of a common nature and of common aims which are above the sphere
of sense,—of a nature and aims existing independently of the
mutable objects with which they are conversant, ever reveals a
seat of power above the world and not of the world, a spiritual fastness, from which more mightily than from the coveted
stand-point of the Syracusan sage, all men, singly and
jointly, may coerce the things of the world into all the need
ful service of the soul.

Ultimate results   That in the general development and appli-
involved in first   cation of language there is no ground of dis-
principles.   tinction between Mathematics and other sci-

ences may perhaps sufficiently appear from these general remarks thereupon, taken in connection with our previous inquiry into the development of thought in it and them. In all there are evidently degrees of thought corresponding to degrees of experience, whereby the general principles involved in particular facts are found to be nothing less than primary facts in the order of nature, although at the best but secondarily appreciated in the course of investigation and exposition. Like the quinia and morphia of the chemist, they are essential elements of a complete history of nature, although the process of analysis by which they are revealed is a mental rather than a physical one. Their discovery being purely reflective or ideal, and their expression for that simple reason necessarily metaphorical, the more readily they may be thus identified, the more rapidly will the figurative application of terms acquire a literal force, and the poetry of aspiration be followed by the prose of attainment. One branch of knowledge may thus be comparatively prosaic, but the essential history of each alike typifies that of the whole tree. The exploration of the mystical and the annexation of the abstract thus constitute the course of all earnest investigation ; and all science and all literature, so far as they may have escaped, or so fast as they may throw off, the discrepancies and contaminations of misdirected zeal and moral depravity, are thus ever found to verify the familiar couplet of a classic bard,—

> "All are but parts of one stupendous whole,
> Whose body nature is, and GOD the soul."

Rejoice, ye watchers ! at the approaching dawn of that eternal day of truth and freedom, in which all speculation will become science and all science intuition ; and in which mankind will distinguish between prose and poetry, only by their primary functions of communion and praise.

1858.

3 *

NUMBER AS AN OBJECT.

"At any step of Induction, the inductive proposition is a *Theory* with regard to the Facts which it includes, while it is to be looked upon as a *Fact* with respect to the higher generalizations in which it is included. In any other sense the opposition of *Fact* and *Theory* is untenable, and leads to endless perplexity and debate."—Dr. Whewell.

"Time, time only, can gradually wean us from our *Epeolatry*, or word-worship, by spiritualizing our ideas of the thing signified. Man is an idolater or symbol-worshiper by nature, . . . but sooner or later all his local and temporary symbols must be ground to powder, like the golden calf,—word-images as well as metal or wooden ones. Rough work,—iconoclasm,—but the only way to get at truth."—Dr. Holmes.

CONSEQUENT upon the too natural confusion of things with thoughts on the one hand, and of thoughts with words on the other, is the natural tendency of traditional philosophy to lapse from the firm ground of observation into the delusive quicksands of speculation. Except as our human nature is continually inspired by a Wisdom higher than its own, to a continual refinement, both of thought and of language, it is evident that we must corrupt the universal system of truth by the infusing of individual peculiarities, or mar it by the imputing of individual limitations, in all our efforts to systematize our ever accumulating stores of intellectual attainment. The philosophy of Aristotle may be said to have thus become engulfed in the absurdities of the mediæval schools; while the profounder system of Plato has survived only to meet a like fate in the extravagances of modern rationalism. More justly than those of many professed followers, may the

labors of BACON, and LOCKE, and many other less appreciated
observers and inquirers of modern times, be regarded as sup-
plementary, and not antagonistic, to those of the ancient mon-
archs of mind, in recalling the attention of mankind from
tradition to experience, from criticism to investigation, from
words to things.

Things or objects are the proper subject of all study and of
all teaching. Let us however avoid the too common error of
confusing an object, with an aim. An object is properly
something which is at hand : an aim is something which is
ever, in some sense, at a distance. The aim of an intelligent
and spiritual being is nothing less than the inexhaustible treasure of divine Truth. A demonstrable object is a part of his
present wealth of knowledge, although as such also a means
of future acquisition. Objects are the only proper, because
the only possible, subjects of investigation and demonstration.
Surely it is an evidence that the intellect of our age had wan-
dered far into the wilderness of self-conceit, that the plan of
object-teaching should be announced to us almost as a discovery, and welcomed by us as a refreshing novelty. In the
motion of the mind as in that of the body, the headlong attitude
is unfavorable to safe progress. In both we must plant our
feet firmly upon the earth of tangible realities, if we would
have the free use of all our faculties.

In speaking of objects, we of course mean in the first place
objects of sensation, as these must be our first means of communication, either with young people, or with others who
may not have undergone a mental training similar to our own,
so as to become familiar with the intellectual objects, or ideas,
which we may have derived from these. Of these objects of
sensation, which may thus be called primary objects in the
order of experience, I now purpose to speak of one which I
think must sooner or later be taught more simply and accurately, and therefore of course more efficiently than it now is.
I mean the object of Number, which we are more accus-
tomed to hear spoken of as a deduction or creation of the in-

tellect, than as a sensible quality of matter. For the sake of perspicuity, let us premise the consideration of this subject with a glance at another more undisputed quality of matter, and object of sensation.

The object of Color may be taken as a representative quality of matter, although, like all the rest, it depends for its manifestation upon the subtler and more diffused medium in which the principles of light, heat, attraction, repulsion, and polarity, appear to meet and blend. Color, we know, may either belong to a mass or masses of matter naturally, or be imparted by art. The same is evidently true of Number; and although the quality of Number may be doubtless imparted or altered with greater facility than that of Color, I cannot think that this is a sufficient plea for our laying claim to its idea as a creation or original endowment of the intellect. Similar remarks might be made upon the idea of Space, and to some extent upon that of Time; but let us now proceed to consider how this view of our knowledge of Number may concern the teacher of the science of Numbers.

The few remarks which I have to offer on this question, if novel, will not I trust seem unpractical, nor if simple, trifling, to those who know the craving of the youthful and untutored mind for original knowledge, and the inhumanity of offering a stone to the son who asks for bread.

In the first place then, it may be observed that as the idea of Number exists in the mind as a part of memory, so the combinations of numbers are essentially mere matters of memory. We remember that two and two make four, just as we remember that blue and yellow make green; but we cannot conceive of a numerous nothing, any more than of a colored nothing. When therefore the pupil demands of the teacher his authority for saying that two and two make four, or that a whole is greater than a part, the teacher may wisely refrain from replying that the doctrine is a self-evident truth, apart from its application to matter. By basing his assertion wholly on the ground of observation, by contenting himself, for instance, with showing that two sticks and two sticks make four sticks, he may both guard his pupil from the presumption of more than mortal independence of intellect, and himself from the danger of being requested to explain how, upon conceded mathematical principles, two and two make forty, or an hundred, as truly as they make four, if the numbers do not refer to anything.

Another result of this view of the origin of our knowledge of Number, is a consistent theory of the intellectual processes of Multiplication and Division. Although, for instance, 25 times 25, if the multiplicand be considered a merely abstract number, are equal to nothing; and although 25 cents cannot be multiplied by 25 cents, as a late eminent teacher remarked, any more than 25 lawyers by 25 bears, yet 25 cents may be multiplied by 25, as surely as one cent may be, and without any danger of our being at a loss to decide whether the result is 6¼ cents, or $6.25. Here again the labor of intellect, being confined to perception, recollection and inference, without any recourse to the hypothetical postulates which have heretofore been so largely made the basis of mathematical science, enables all to unite intelligently on the firm ground of natural truth. There is hypothesis of course in every movement of the intellect. In the present case both the more concrete multiplicand and the more abstract multiplier, are hypotheses, as the result is also an hypothesis until it shall be realized in some external negotiation. But inasmuch as the operation is not ostensibly based upon hypothesis, we may thus far at least avoid countenancing the too often convenient doctrine, that there are fields of knowledge in which it is our right and duty to be unintelligible. How can any doctrine be essentially unintelligible, in which the teacher may have followed the example of the beloved disciple and veteran apostle of the LORD CHRIST, in proclaiming only that which his eyes have seen and his hands have handled, of the object which is his subject?

C

CURRENT ARITHMETIC.

" That which is wanting cannot be numbered."—ECCLES. i. •6

MY ciphering is strange work, I find.
   I first take nothings, and in sport
Pretend them somethings. In my mind
   I count them, till I cut them short,

And say, So many. Then some more
   I take, and mix with them, and call
It ADDING. Or to stint my store,
   I say SUBTRACT a part from all.

Such sport is this Arithmetic!
   My nothing-somethings thus at will
I call to mind, and, sparse or thick,
   By pure pretence arrange them still.

But one thing more :—as I enact,
   I still remember what I do :
I COUNT, I ADD, and I SUBTRACT,
   I order, and keep all in view.

In added addings, I pretend,
   I have a helper close at hand :
A counted counter is this friend,
   To MULTIPLY at my command.

And in repeated stintings, too,
   By like invention or pretence,
I find a friend like work to do,
   DIVIDING, less in fact than sense.

And so are all the other rules
   Which fag the faculties of youth,
Like all the cant of all the schools,
   Partly pretence, and partly truth.

THE HOUSE OF BONDAGE.

"THE earnest expectation of the creation waits for the revelation of the sons of God. Because the creation has been subject to vanity, not willingly, but by reason of Him who made it subject in hope. For the creation itself will also be set free from the servitude of corruption, into the glorious freedom of the children of God. Forasmuch as we know, that all the creation both groans and is in labor together until now. Not only so, but also ourselves, who have the first fruit of the Spirit, even we ourselves groan in ourselves, waiting for the adoption, the redemption of our body."—ROM. viii. 19–23.

PANTHEISM and Transcendentalism are terms of modern date, which, belonging rather to the history of groping speculation, than to that of definite progress in doctrine, must convey to the mind of the general reader but a vague or a doubtful meaning. Perhaps they may be most distinctly defined by saying that Pantheism is the doctrine or heresy which confounds GOD with the created universe, and Transcendentalism that which confounds Man with it. Perhaps it may also be safely said that the two are fused together into the most subtle form of practical Atheism, by a third heresy, which has received the name of Rationalism, and which consists essentially in the confusion, still more glaringly absurd when thus separately stated, of the omniscient and prescient Creator with the ignorant though percipient creature. Of the three, Transcendentalism is evidently the doctrine or assumption which approaches nearest to being an aspect of universal truth or experience, since the external universe is practically found, as well as divinely promised, to be the servant of man, so far as man is master of himself. It is chiefly the want of a due regard to this condition of self-mastery or self-subjection, resulting from a want of appreciation of the crucifying discipline through which only it can be truly attained, which makes the doctrine taught under that name unsound and impracticable. We can all see the point of the friendly satire in which its most famous representative has been depicted, as one

> "In whose eyes all creation is duly respected,
>   As parts of himself, just a little projected ;"

but it is no less evident that the conquest of external nature is an unceasing result of the continuous march of intellect, which again is equally seen in an enlarged view of history, to follow the spread of the religion of self-denial. "Man," says the ingenious author* of *The Sexuality of Nature*, "is nature concentrated ; Nature, man diffused." There is evidently a sense in which the outward creation as a whole increasingly becomes a sort of social, dividual body to the general human mind, however the believers in an unregenerate "self-respect" may fall short in its attempted possession. Thus far therefore we may recognize an element of truthfulness in the assumptions of Transcendentalism, without accepting its crude extravagances, or at all committing ourselves to the support of the associated delusions of Pantheism and Rationalism. A few words of acknowledgment are here due to our authority for the somewhat transcendental variation from the common version of the above cited extract from the Epistle to the Romans.

Little appears to be known of Anthony Purver, except the history of his Translation of the Bible. Of the work itself almost as little is known even to his successors in religious profession.† There is ground for believing that the fruits of his industry in that labor of love have not yet been received

---

* Leopold Hartley Grindon.
† Of the Society of Friends.

by the religious and literary world with the appreciation
which they deserve ; but as the triumphs of truth and justice
are ever rendered more complete by delay, we may regard
this circumstance without regret, on account either of the
work or of the workman. " He who believeth maketh not
haste," because in and through faith he has " the substance
of things hoped for." With the qualification of a scholarship
which was rather profound than general or promiscuous, our
Friend seems to have brought to his work a zeal for literal
accuracy, which was alike removed from a superstitious reverence for his materials, and from a presumptuous confidence
in his own powers of interpretation. He often calls our
attention to instances in which the same word, occurring in
different parts of the original text, has been diversely rendered in our authorized version, at the discretion or caprice
of the translators ; thus perhaps indicating his conviction that
the simple language of pure inspiration needs not, nor admits
of the gloss of an artificial variety. But in one remarkable
instance he deviates, in this respect, both from the original
Scripture and from other versions. He presumes, for once,
to suggest that the original utterance may not have been sufficiently explicit for all time. When the apostle Peter, after
telling us to " honor all men," specifically enjoins upon us to
" honor the king," he thinks that this is not enough, and is
constrained to say " reverence the king," by way of increasing
the distinction. In this latter half of the Nineteenth Century
such scrupulosity may probably seem superfluous to readers
on either side of the Atlantic Ocean ; but we may at least
honor the independence of thought which proceeded from
such loyalty, as his doubtless was, to the political sovereignty
under which he flourished. Our opening text is given according to Purver's Translation, and may be regarded as a fair
specimen of his literal fidelity.

" The land of Egypt, the house of bondage" of which we
so often read in the record of the dealings of Almighty GOD
with his chosen people under the patriarchal and Mosaic dis-

pensations, is an impressive type of the spiritual condition in which all the children of Adam enter into the world, and in which they must at the best remain, except as " the spirit of bondage" may be exchanged for " the spirit of adoption." The power of Him who came to bruise the head of the Serpent, and his power alone, is still able, as joined with, to remove the curse of the fall in its individual application, and to restore us "from the servitude of corruption to the glorious freedom of the children of GOD."

As the apostle elsewhere writes, " whilst we are at home in the body, we are absent from the LORD ;" and it is accordingly natural for the carnal mind to forget its divine Author and Benefactor. In making idols of the riches of creation, we may thus practically and even avowedly deny the only Creator ; but we will not find that such false devotion can secure us from the power of evil. A much-admired poetess,[*] whose voice is but lately hushed, has sadly sung,

"The fool hath said, There is no GOD,
But none, There is no sorrow."

Disappointments, vexations and perplexities are sure to assail and oppress the soul which is not redeemed from all reliance upon objects of sense and upon merely human sympathy, through the indwelling of " the Spirit of Him that raised up Jesus from the dead." That merely human " favor is deceitful," as merely outward " beauty is vain," is a confession which has been attributed to one whose knowledge of the world was not to be surpassed ; and the lesson is confirmed to us by the testimony of the apostle of love, who ranks " the pride of life" and " the lust of the eye" with the groveling " lust of the flesh," declaring that they all " are not of the Father, but of the world." Whatever may be our worldly advantages, if we turn away from the offers of the Divine Grace which alone is sufficient for us, and which can always

* ELIZABETH BARRETT BROWNING.

adapt our desires to our circumstances, we make ourselves the slaves of our circumstances, and tools of the Evil Power, who through them seeks to blind our spiritual vision. The whole creation may thus become a " a house of bondage" to the soul which regards not the importunity of the Holy Spirit, and which despises the seeming weakness of the cross of Christ. On the other hand, the whole creation will assuredly become a temple of liberty and gladness and 'praise, " a new heavens and a new earth" beyond the reach of " the second death," to all who by a faithful submission and adherence to the terms of salvation "obtain a part in the first resurrection." Whatever the worldly disadvantages of these may seem to be, they will at least be always the contented masters of their circumstances, and triumphant in them over the wiles of Satan and of human adversaries.

We read that during the plague of darkness which overtook their oppressors, " the Children of Israel had light in their dwellings." So, in the perfect dispensation in which all transient types are permanently fulfilled, the singleness of vision, which consists in an unreserved and uncalculating devotion to duty, is the prescribed condition upon which alone our whole bodies may be filled with light. Imaginations and inventions are of no avail for the attainment of this signal blessing. Both the individual culture, which is grounded on the mere love of what we may call beauty, and the officious action which aims even at the welfare of our brethren otherwise than as an object secondary to the discharge of our own spiritual calling, must be regarded as mere refinements of selfishness and self-assertion. We may thus wander into Unitarian license on the one hand and into Romish supererogation on the other ; but the cross of Christ, as immediately revealed and adapted to the need of every soul by the Holy Spirit, is the one universal and undeceitful rule of duty for fallen man, and the simple means of that union with GOD and with one another, whereby we may realize in all our actions the efficiency and harmony of true freedom. A true sympathy with our fellow-men will doubtless lead us to seek every refinement of their mental and physical condition, and every enlargement of their opportunities for action, which their constitutional sensibilities may fit them for. Surely, the world affords no nobler object of pursuit! But is there no danger of our stooping in bondage to "the beggarly elements" even in such a work as this? As subjects of the spiritual and perfect dispensation of the Gospel, are we not bound to teach and exemplify the entire subordination of the resources of nature to those of grace, through all the diversities of inherited and acquired character and condition? Let us then beware of allowing our zeal to overrule our knowledge, and by placing sentiment before experience or philanthropy before religion, to confirm our inherited bondage, seeing that "there remaineth no more sacrifice for sin," to the victims of the second death.

THE LAW OF THE ROAD.

"Be of one mind."—1 Cor. i. 10; 2 Cor. xiii. 11., Etc.

HEAVEN is the reward of faithful labor. It is the rest from labor, and the completion of labor, so far as labor involves struggle and strife; although it may be called the very beginning of action, so far as action is animated by that divine harmony of pure strength and perfect fitness, through which alone activity becomes entirely effectual and fruitful. In either case the knowledge of this divine harmony implies the knowledge of God, which is life eternal; and the increase of it which God, through Christ, and by the Spirit, works in the souls of his earnest seekers and submissive children, is the true promotion of his glory. The salvation of their own souls, and the glory of their Creator, are thus practically one object in the aspirations of Christians.

The Eternal being the only ground and foundation of the Temporal, the unseen world of course supplies the principles through which alone the agencies and circumstances of outward life can be reconciled with one another, or appreciated and applied in the simplicity which the unity of truth requires. This is obviously what some writers who are called transcendental mean, when they teach that the supernatural is more important and more real, while no less present, than the natural. Through the inherited infirmity which the pride of acquired learning and power cannot ignore, we are naturally more prone to the investigation of the superficial than of the profound, and have to arrive at our knowledge of force only through our experience of form. We are born as it were upon the surface of things, the first birth being that of the flesh, and not that of the spirit. We are naturally fragmentary and impotent, although seemingly independent, individuals; but we are called to become sympathizing members of a dividual fellowship, in which the will is free because it is one and comprehensive, while the actions are dependent because they are manifold and comprehended. The natural, or individual and divided, is our appointed road to the supernatural, or dividual and united. The Christian pilgrimage is that by which we must travel from the state of nature to the state of grace, if we ever become true Christians.

Labor is of three kinds or degrees. There is the labor of the heart or of the soul, the labor of the head or of the mind, and the labor of the hands and auxiliary muscles and members. The diversities of human labor, like all other healthy diversities, have indeed their common principle of unity, and that principle is here the action of the human will. Involuntary or unconscious habit is not labor, any more than are the changes of the so-called inanimate elements of nature, which represent no other life than the will of their omnipresent Creator. The three kinds of labor may therefore be said to be manifested, so far as they can be manifested, the first in motives or dispositions; the second, in original thoughts; and the third, in voluntary actions, or adopted habits.

In dealing with our fellow men we are constantly called upon to pass judgment upon their performances, as our only alternative from passing judgment upon themselves. Their dispositions and intentions are a part of themselves; their expressions and actions are the fruits which they impart for our probation and possible benefit, whether they are so designed by them or not. These, therefore, it is our duty to attend to and to deal with, according to our own views of their value and applicability. As external facts, they are the natural *media* of communion through which all who recognize the permanent principles of the internal life, may test the degrees of their relationship in those ties of intellect, which may be said to be intermediate to the strictly external and the strictly internal regions of experience. As it is those only who have laid hold of permanent principles, who can truly think originally or for themselves, original thoughts must imply honest hearts; and the extent to which such can agree in the estimation of external events, is the measure of their ability to sympathize and co-operate in the work of the world. An inability to agree in thought in regard to the facts of our joint experience, evidently implies either a want of the singleness of purpose which an earnest belief in the unity of principles supplies, or a latent and constitutional diversity in mental prepossession or the habits of thought. The one of these difficulties must be, and the other may be, an insuperable barrier to our uniting in labor as lovers of truth.

Since, however, union or fellowship is the noblest object of labor with which this world supplies us, and may indeed be said to be the very experience which connects the life of earth with that of heaven, it becomes and ever remains our duty to do all that we can to surmount whatever barriers we may find in the way of its increasing realization. And as true union is that only which proceeds from the fellowship of spirit, this is the standard by which all subordinate forms of fellowship are to be estimated. As similarity of action is not desirable save as it proceeds from and implies similarity of opinion, so neither is similarity of opinion, save as it implies similarity of feeling. As has, however, already been observed, similarity of opinion is a measure or test of the degree of fellowship which honest hearts can maintain in action: and since, in the exercise of the charity which " believes all things," we are bound to presume that our fellows, in whatever depth of darkness and depravity they may have been sunk by external influences or by their own previous transgressions, are at least for the present honest in their pursuit of good, similarity of opinion may be regarded as the single goal to which our efforts at fellowship should be practically directed.   The manifestation of opinions in actions is indefinitely modified and masked by varying circumstances; and our feelings are naturally inappreciable to others save as they are embodied and communicated in opinions and actions. Fellowship, therefore, in the purely external, being comparatively unattainable, and in the purely internal comparatively inappreciable, the intermediate or intellectual region of experience remains, as that in which we must in the first place strive to unite, if we aim at a fellowship which may be at once feasible and fruitful.   Our law of intercourse is thus indicated both by its own propriety, and by the exclusion of others which might be rashly adopted as more practicable or more refined.

The Present may be styled our road to the Future, as the External is to the Internal.   The two journeys may be regarded as one, and the same rules may be recognized as the guides of our pilgrimage in each.   Human fellowship must be regarded in each as the strongest support and the noblest object, after the pure communion with the divine Author of our being.   The surest instrumental agency, as we have now seen, by which we can promote this fellowship, is the labor of intellect.   It becomes us, in the next place, to seek to perform that labor with the independence which proceeds from true earnestness, and with the prudence which proceeds from true humility.

Assuming, as we must, the unity of truth, we may infer that the only effectual labor of intellect is that which tends to realize that unity, by an ever growing appreciation of its profound importance.   If we thus realize it for ourselves, and subsequently find that it has been realized by others, we so discover a ground of union between ourselves and them.   But if we begin by assuming a ground of union with any to whom we may capriciously wish to be attached, and seek accord-

ingly to conform our opinions to what we may conceive theirs
to be, we must evidently be living at best upon a borrowed
faith, which will lack strength if it do not also lack sound-
ness, and which will be sure to desert us, if it do not destroy
us, in the inevitable time of trial. In the one case we pursue
the path of wisdom ; in the other, that of folly. Their marks
are easily distinguishable when thus brought into contrast. It
behooves every one to bear in mind the simple difference between them, and to be upon the watch to confirm the good,
and to reform the evil, in his own character and career. As
each one is busied with thinking upon his own duties, he will
not be in danger of attributing imaginary thoughts to other
people, either to their annoyance or for his own delusion.
The truth is happily so inexhaustible in its grandeur and .
loveliness, that its earnest votaries will value even the delights
of human fellowship, but as brooks by the way, while pressing
forward to the perfect union in the Father's house of " many
mansions," which is built upon the Rock, IMMANUEL.

ATONEMENT.

THE word once spoken may not be recalled:
   Time past may not return :
How shall the forfeit be forestalled
   To justice stern ?

I wring my hands and gnash my teeth in vain!
   In view of my mistake,
I seem to feel the mark of CAIN,
   And fear and quake.

And still I struggle to restore the debt ;
   Alas ! new debts arise,
From new-found duties pressing yet
   On me unwise.

Dread taskmaster ! by thee, O Law ! I die,
   Except some miracle
My lack of service shall supply,
   And speed me well.

Were once the mischief of the past removed,
   My life, from tumult free,
Might journey in the path approved,
   Not hopelessly.

Then should I know a GOD of strength and will
   To meet my present need,
And ready with conducting skill
   My course to speed.

Spring, Holy Fount of healing love ! for such
   Our fathers say Thou art ;
And cleanse with thy sufficient touch
   My leprous heart !

THE LAND OF PROMISE.

"THOU shalt no more be termed Forsaken, neither shall thy land be any more termed Desolate: but thou shalt be called Hephzibah, and thy land Beulah: for the LORD delighteth in thee, and thy land shall be married."— ISA. lxii. 4.

THE last seven chapters of the Book of the Evangelical Prophet vividly portray the doom of the self-deluded voluptuary, as contrasted with the reward of the self-denying believer in the work and merits of the only Saviour. As the denial of self ensures a devotion to the demands of duty, by simply suppressing the disposition to idle indulgence which is natural to man, CHRIST crucified is found to be ever "the power of GOD and the wisdom of GOD" to all who lift their affections from "the things which perish with the using," "desiring to be clothed upon with their house not made with hands, eternal in the heavens." The cross of CHRIST, being proposed to us as an universal rule of life, evidently renders all compromise impossible between the pursuit of pleasure and that of duty, leaving, indeed, the impure pleasure which is sought and found for its own sake, as a heritage of corruption to those who despise its discipline, but opening ever new sources of happiness to those who value pleasure merely as the handmaid of duty. The antagonism between pleasure and duty is one which has originated in sin, and which subsists only in the "evil heart of unbelief." In the experience of the regenerate Christian, they are reconciled "both unto GOD in one body by the Cross," which alone is able as submitted to, to keep the love of the reward in its proper subordination to the love of the work, and to induce a neglect of earthly enjoyment save as it may be the attendant of faithful performance. Duty being followed as the only object and the only law of life, so far as any object and law are needed other than the love of GOD and of our fellow-men, pleasure will be found at our side as a faithful and useful ally in the work of righteousness, and beauty will not lag far behind. The principle of enmity being thus slain in ourselves, the occasion of enmity with one another will also be removed, and all feelings of division and distance will be superseded by those of fellowship and attraction, as we steadily advance to the goal of heavenly union in the Divine Centre and Source of all good.

The charity or love which never fails, may be said to be represented in human character by the three subordinate and co-ordinate traits, of humility, simplicity, and activity; which, again, are respectively manifested in outward life by the fruits of concord, intelligence, and progress. As neither of these traits can be the genuine offspring of the faith which works by love, except as it is accompanied by the others, so the fruits which severally indicate them can actually exist only in combination. Either the concord, or the intelligence, or the progress, seeming to exist alone, must be a mere seeming which is superficial, unsound, and futile. Existing together, they certify a happy approach to that only worthy object of all labor and aspiration, the realization of the Divine Presence by a participation in the divine perfections. "LORD, Thou hast been our dwelling-place in all generations," was the devout acknowledgment of the Jewish leader and lawgiver, uttered, doubtless, in the intense appreciation of individual insignificance, of social importance, and of filial efficiency for every good word and work, which the view of himself, of his fellows, and of the world, in the light of divine revelation, could not fail to supply. In accordance with this are the words of ELIHU, "There is a spirit in man, and the inspiration of the Almighty giveth them understanding;" and those of King SOLOMON, " GOD hath made man upright, but they have sought out many inventions." The occasion of all our delusions may be said to lie in the peculiarities which attach to our individual life, in consequence of our ancestral fall. Only when we feel, and think, and act, as man, and not as men or individuals, do we observe or regain the integrity of our original nature. Despising that spiritual simplicity of truth and good which can in our fallen estate be realized only by the power of faith, and thinking to know good exclusively or pre-eminently for ourselves, we reject the path of true discovery for that of delusive invention. Then indeed are we "taken captive by the Devil at his will," relying upon show as if it were substance, and confirming ourselves by the example of others who may be like-minded with us, instead of accepting the offered guidance of the only infallible SPIRIT. Then do we lay ourselves open to the apostolic admonition, " I fear lest by any means as the serpent beguiled EVE through his subtlety, so your minds should be corrupted from the simplicity that is in CHRIST." But as we individually wait for " the inspiration of the Almighty," to make us truly acquainted with the spirit of man, and with all its wants, and with its true relations to the Spirit of GOD, it becomes possible for the empty arrogance, the blinding confusion, and the specious slothfulness of spirit, which betray the continued presence of the old Serpent in the world, to be replaced by the stable dignity, the enlightening simplicity, and the genuine activity of Divine Love.

The life of true work is one with the life of true faith. The author of the Epistle to the Hebrews, after writing that " Faith is the substance of things hoped for, and the evidence of things not seen," has added, " Without faith it is impossible to please God : for he that cometh to God must believe that He is, and that He is a rewarder of them that diligently seek Him." This soul-satisfying conviction is doubtless both the preliminary stimulus, and the growing consequence, as

5   D

well as the sure test, of an earnest, working faith. The apostle PAUL testified to his "son in the faith," that "godliness,
with contentment, is great gain, having the promise of the
life which now is, and of that which is to come." And the
same eminent authority elsewhere appeals to "that holy
Spirit of promise, which is the earnest of our inheritance
until the redemption of the purchased possession." As this
Spirit of promise can only be apprehended by faith, the exercise of faith consisting indeed in nothing more or less than
the effectual apprehension of its holy help, it follows that a
true faith implies a measurable realization through it of the
Heavenly Life. Faith and its consequence being thus practically inseparable, we may understand how the inspired
penman, without deviating from the ordinary and necessary
license of language, happened to write of faith as being itself " the substance of things hoped for, and the evidence of
things not seen." His object was doubtless not so much accurately to define a doctrine, in advance of the then prevailing
development of thought, as efficiently to commend a practice ;
and his words were clearly neither too few, nor too many, nor
illy chosen, for the occasion. The important doctrine which
the militant Church is now perhaps preparing to maintain with
increasing precision, is, that true working faith, the " obedience of faith" as distinguished from the " assurance of faith,"
is simply that right exercise of the human will, or power of
spiritual choice, which is necessary for the reception of the
freely offered salvation. It is the voluntary submission to the
drawings of that Spirit of the FATHER of spirits, which is at
once the Spirit of judgment and the Spirit of promise. The
salvation which comes by faith is indeed the gift of GOD in
CHRIST our only Atonement and Mediator ; but the work of
faith must in an individual sense, begin in ourselves, although
that beginning may consist but in the willing realization of
our own impotence. Only as it thus begins can it be hoped
to result in that experimental communion with the FATHER
which leads to the realization of his heavenly promises, and

the fulfillment of his perfect will, through the birth of that love, and the nourishment of that hope, which are the guide and the support of the regenerated soul.

Many indeed are the occasional promises which are recorded for the encouragement of those who seek an heavenly country. The riches which the Almighty Creator can and will bestow upon his obedient children, are doubtless as boundless as are his mercies to the repentant sinner; and lest the sinner should want a motive to repent, he is even repeatedly reminded that the very revenues of the wicked shall become the heritage of the just. But a written assurance is of merely secondary value to those who have realized the spiritual substance through an immediate acquaintance with the Word inwardly revealed. May we so enter by the door of faith into the synagogue of our own hearts, as ever to hear the voice of Him whose wont it is to be there in the midst, while He proclaims, " This day is this Scripture fulfilled in your ears !" Luke iv. 21.

THE PLACE OF FICTION.

"No man seweth a piece of new cloth on an old garment."—MARK ii. 21.

IT is worthy of remark that the contrast between Fact and Fiction is less definite than that between Truth and Falsehood. Fact, being distinctively the embodiment of Truth or knowledge, and Fiction, that of Falsehood or ignorance, they are of course practically distinguishable from each other, only so far as we may succeed in tracing actions or impressions to the determining principles of character. Fiction, therefore, as a most frequent if not universal element of human performance or experience, becomes a matter of immediate practical interest to all earnest thinkers, in its diverse relations to Truth or essential good, and to Falsehood, or essential evil.

So far as human knowledge is conjectural, all thought, it is evident, must partake of the nature of fiction. So long as human systems of doctrine, even though progressive in their tendency, shall be fragmentary in themselves, they must themselves be obviously fictions as compared with the unseen but undoubted perfect system to which they tend. We can conceive that our rudimentary thoughts and systems of thought might be faultless as well as progressive ; and then we might infer that our own starting-point was the merely negative condition of ignorance. It is the circumstance that we can accept no revelations of GOD or of external nature as a whole, that is, without the consciousness of subjective imperfections, or deficiencies of perception, which must be either

52

left void in our thought, or bridged over by hypothesis, which betrays the ravages of sin in our intellectual constitution, and corroborates the outward traditional revelation that our starting-point is the darkness of positive unbelief. Thus, in substance, does every earnest soul, in the light of the Spirit which "helpeth our infirmities," demonstrate to itself the necessity of the faith or heart-belief, of which it is testified that "the just shall live"* by it, and also that the system and substance of divine truth, or the "righteousness of GOD," is "revealed from faith to faith,"* that is, progressively. The element of fiction, and the trace of falsehood, though unconsciously inhering in every private system of faith, until faith is itself lost in sight, meanwhile steadily decreases so far as the soldier of faith is himself concerned, though ever of course gaining fresh entrance into the conquests which he bequeaths to his still struggling companions and successors.

From the very constitution of human nature, therefore, fiction is an inseparable element of social life. Individuals may have systems of faith without actually putting faith in their systems. They may escape delusion as their faith may be the leader rather than the follower of their system. But as corporations are said to have no souls, so society in general has no conscience. The social standard is but a sort of average of individual standards, and social progress, of individual progress. Every one therefore who mingles in human society must encounter Fiction, either as victor or as victim. His destiny takes the direction of his faith. If this shall be but "to himself before God," he will with the best of reason "be fully persuaded in his own mind," and will tend to rise above conventional fiction, even while using it for conventional purposes. If on the other hand any one shall surrender his faith to a clique, a system or a vocabulary, he is sure to "condemn himself in that thing which he alloweth." The infinite capacity commits itself to a finite aim. "The man

* ROM. i. 17.

5 *

falls down "* to an unworthy object, and as he persists, the loss must be indeed "past retrieving." The all-significant if not all-important province of language, being itself wholly a growth of fiction, naturally furnishes the most abundant illustrations of the course of character in either direction. "By thy words thou shalt be justified, and by thy words thou shalt be condemned," said the Incarnate Word,† and the testimony of the President of the Apostles may be similarly construed, ‡ "If any man offend not in word, the same is a perfect man."

As Sir JAMES MACKINTOSH has profoundly observed, there is a special talent of expression to every order of thought. "Those," said he, "who content themselves with the common speculations of their age, generally possess the talent of expressing them, which must have been pretty widely diffused before the speculations became common." Even by comparatively superficial thinkers, if but truly circumspect livers, the universal allegory of language may doubtless be safely and profitably, though mechanically or semi-unconsciously applied, since, as has been often suggested, truth, like corn, has to be consumed and lived upon, and must, to some extent be sacrificed, so to speak, in the process,—the license of custom serving as a foil to the otherwise dangerous two-edged sword, on the theoretical side. But a nobler application, a deeper work of faith, which is comparable to the planting of the seed-corn, is that in which the same celebrated thinker proceeds to show that the previous application is found to be fictitious :—" But there are times when there is a general tendency toward something higher, and when no man has quite reached the objects, still less the subsequent and auxiliary powers of expression. In these intervals between one mode of thinking and another, literature seems to

---

* " Little were the change of station, loss of life or crown ;
But the wreck were past retrieving, if the man fell down."
LOWELL, *Mahmood.*

† MATT. xii. 37.   ‡ JAM. iii. 2.

decline, while mind is really progressive, because no one has acquired the talent of the new manner of thinking."

Fictitious narrative, or avowed romance, can of course only have a legitimate sphere and function, so far as professedly veracious history or biography may fail to reflect the essential eʰements of actual life in their natural fullness, and just relations of proportion and perspective. Beyond the limits of this want, it must evidently at best be but a secondary and distorted reflection of nature, adapted only to the imaginary demands of those inferior and sectarian orders of character and intellect. to which sincerity is repulsive, and truth terrible.

ROMANCE.

OUR common life is creeping prose :
    We heap our ant-hills high,
Exultant that our puny toes
    Should so sublimely fly.

For how can common life ascend
    Above the things of earth,
Or on the baseless dreams depend
    Which poets bring to birth ?

Upon what common ground, think you,
    Must men converse or band ?
Except what lies beneath their view,
    What can they understand ?

This nether world alone is ours :
    Weak children of the clay,
What boots it to inflate our powers,
    To reach the orb of day ?

Yet at our daylight's frequent close,
    See duty's stars grow bright,
The members of the mind repose,
    And faith extend its flight.

Then dreams of beauty find a place :
    The sternest heart succumbs,
And for a season gains the grace
    To feed on heavenly crumbs.

Oh, tell me of some larger life,
    E'en now on earth begun,
Where truth and beauty drop their strife,
    And rise and rule as one !

THE DRIFT OF SYNTAX.

" Day unto day uttereth speech."—Ps. xix. 2.

THE iceberg is the child of the snow-flake. Its gradual growth, its formidable progress, and its sudden dissolution, as now observed and understood, alike illustrate the definite action of gentle, but irresistible and all-pervading influences, and clearly indicate that all that is yet unaccountable in meteorology and cosmology may be attributed to the vastness of the field yet to be explored, rather than to any essential obscurity of the determining principles.

The field of Language, no less than that of physical research, abounds in interesting monuments of the gradual and silent operation of almost inappreciable influences. Though the world of mind, which here comes into view, is indisputably deeper than that of matter, yet for this element of difficulty the explorer has at least the compensating encouragement, that inasmuch as he is only dealing with the relics of past thought, he is only attempting to retrace a progress which has been proved possible under circumstances of observation less favorable than his own.

The elements of language may be broadly divided into the impersonal and the personal. As it is the office of human speech merely to express human knowledge and communicable experience, of course it can suggest the Deity only secondarily, or so far as He may be at once symbolized outwardly in his creation, and known inwardly in our experience. There can therefore obviously be no immediately

divine element in language, except such as it may share with
other phenomena of more purely natural origin. Things
and people, Nature and Man, as the immediate subjects of all
speech, are the material of all suggestions, and the basis of all
inferences, which can by it be conveyed from mind to mind.

It is obvious that the personal element of language must
distinctively consist in the expression or attribution of action
and feeling. The expression or attribution of mere being, on
the other hand, is more closely limited,—and with increasing
closeness by the advance of general science,—to things, and
to human character in its universal or impersonal aspect.
As personal views or aims avowedly prevail, therefore, verbs
of volition and consciousness will be the prominent members
of a sentence ; and, as impersonal interests are discovered,
and pursued or professed, nouns substantive, and the so-called
substantive verb, " to be."

Since all intelligent communication presupposes a basis of
mutual intelligence, there are always some words in a sentence which will be more apt to be anticipated by the hearer
as being suggested by the others, than those others would be
if left to the latter part or end of the sentence. Whether,
therefore, the personal or the impersonal standard of interest
and ground of understanding shall prevail between speaker
and hearer, the hearer's power of attention will be best econo-
mized, and his stock of interest most surely maintained or increased, by leaving the more matter-of-course, though con-
ventionally, or even intrinsically, more important words, to
the last. As the fixing of the point implies the content of
the intellectual pyramid,* the care will be first to satisfy the

---

* By the use, indeed, of the substantive verb in combination with partici-
ples or infinitives in place of the personal moods, every sentence may be con-
verted into a sort of equation in which the logical copula, "is," corresponds
to the mathematical sign of equality, =. But where an agent is concerned,
the subject must be either of greater or less acknowledged consequence than
the logical predicate, according as the aim of the narrative or argument is the
glory of the individual, or the illustration of abstract truth. In this case,
therefore, instead of a suspended balance, the sentence may be compared to

thirst for information with the formal little, and afterward the sense of grammatical completeness with the formal much. The prevailing structure of the sentence, in a particular community or at a particular era, thus becomes an index of the prevailing creed of life, as implied in the pre-supposed basis of common intelligence. Where, as among the old Romans, virtue is practically, as well as etymologically, identified with mere manliness, the tendency to hero-worship inevitably shows itself in the customary gravitation of the verb to the bottom of the sentence. Where good, and the Source of good, are sought in things or principles, rather than in people, as to some extent in the less worldly-minded, though more ancient Greeks, and more largely and avowedly in the more modern professors of Christianity, the human element is less developed, or shrinks into comparative insignificance by the side of that which more immediately and purely symbolizes the Creative, and Sustaining, and "Unspeakable" WORD.

It may be incidentally remarked as being perhaps another result of the defective religion of the great military nation, that in the development of the verb, it seems to have systematically discarded the use of a simple past tense, which has so generally prevailed both among more ancient and more modern peoples. The Imperfect Tense of the Latins, like that of the Greeks before them, was directly expressive only of either continuous or abortive action, and by no means supplied the place either of the Greek Aorist, or of that which

a standing pyramid. If glory be the chase, the aspirations and volitions and subsequent sentiments of the hero (verbs, active or passive) will be more readily anticipated and less eagerly asserted, than the materials (nouns substantive) on which they are exercised, and which, though thus subordinate in secret appreciation, give point, as we say, to the utterance, by indicating that which is then or there novel in the method and results of the life whose highest flight is a homage to circumstances. In the investigation and demonstration of truth, again, the mental or physical movements of the agent are in like manner seen to be at once matters intrinsically of secondary importance, and yet temporarily of more urgent interest, as indicating the method and results of the life which is a continual triumph over circumstances.

in our own tongue has rather capriciously inherited the name
of the Imperfect. The emphatic Perfect was employed by
them for the most part in the wide range of occasions to which
the simple past tense, whether it be called Aorist, or Imperfect, or Preterite, is properly fitted. There is a sort of self-
assertion, or dependence on mere attainment, in their habitual
mention of the past as something which is perfected, which
can perhaps only be accounted for as arising from a theoretical though doubtless ever confusing and often disappointing
dependence on the permanence of worldly interests and institutions. Acknowledging Right only as it was embodied in
successful Might, they were, as a modern observer remarks
of a modern people, " impious in their skepticism of a theory"
which might conflict with their own, but they "would kiss
the dust before a fact." * Foolishness, indeed, to them would
have seemed the boast of the warrior-prophet and king of the
Chosen People, " I have seen an end of all perfection ; but
Thy commandment is exceeding broad."

The vagaries of language are necessarily many, and may
often, in the infancy of the social intellect, rise to the rank
of temporary institutions. But they can never carry the
heart-believer beyond the reach of the voice of GOD in the
soul and in the outward creation ; and all of them must at
last meet and terminate in the universal anthem to which the
Hebrew lyre was so early and happily attuned :

"Praise the LORD from the earth, ye dragons and all deeps :
  Fire, and hail ; snow, and vapors : stormy wind fulfilling his Word :
  Mountains, and all hills ; fruitful trees, and all cedars :
  Beasts, and all cattle ; creeping things, and flying fowl :
  Kings of the earth, and all people ; princes, and all judges of the earth :
  Both young men, and maidens ; old men, and children :
  Let them praise the name of the LORD : for his name alone is excellent ;
  His glory is above the earth and heavens."

* EMERSON ; *English Traits.*

PROPHECY AND INTERPRETATION.

"The word of God is not bound."—2 Tim. ii. 9.

"No prophecy of the Scripture is of its own interpretation."—2 Pet. i. 20.

IT is a remarkable testimony of Lord Bacon respecting some of the prophecies of the Old Testament, that they are "of the nature of their Author, to whom a thousand years are as one day; and therefore they are not fulfilled punctually at once, but have a springing and germinant accomplishment through many ages, though the height or fullness of them may refer to some one age." The power of insight, and that of foresight, will doubtless be twin mysteries so long as the objects of truth upon which they may be exercised shall themselves present any features of apparent incongruity. As the true seat or present origin of all mystery consists merely in the clouded nature of our own perceptions, the rectification of these is of course all that is necessary to exhibit to us in the boundless scenes of the inward and outward creations an ever prevailing coherency. When the true connection of body with spirit, of necessity with freedom, and of time with eternity, shall be intelligently realized, truth will doubtless become in our conceptions the unit which it is in reality; and insight and foresight will become synonymous terms, indicating the sure and ready apprehension, however limited it may be in its reach, of a clear and collected intelligence.

This view of the nature of our own ignorance, and of the secret identity of the unknown with that which we call the known, may not only reconcile to our apprehension the possibility of any alleged degree of intuition or of premonition beyond that which we ourselves may for the time enjoy, but may secure us from rashly discrediting the genuineness of any particular prophetic pretensions on the ground of their being, as it has been termed, " self-fulfilling." The dependence of the future upon the present being recognized as the basis of all prophetical truth, the dependence of a premonition upon a genuine intuition cannot be admitted as an evidence of cunning contrivance on the part of the seer ; but will actually confirm the value of his warnings, however much, by elucidating their mode of origination, it may abate the ignorant awe which may have attributed to him a degree of sanctity and sagacity almost unattainable by mortals. The knowledge of the truth is indeed the great leveler of human distinctions, but it may always be welcomed by the lover of his kind as " a leveler upward."   Well, indeed, might the great jurist of Israel exclaim, " Would GOD that all the LORD's people were prophets !"

If insight and foresight be two names for one power or process, any definite limit of insight must also be a definite limit of foresight. The fullness of any inspiration which may be embodied in words is thus never inexhaustible, because it is always measurable. Prophecy, however, whether it be called insight, or whether foresight, is none the less valuable on account of this limitation, since it is always available as a testimony for the truth to the extent of its original design, and at the same time bears witness, by the very principles of its limitation, as these may be in succession ascertained, to the superior and still more enduring agency and efficacy of the spiritual and divine Word which is the one living Source of its manifold lively streams. This aspect of the subject appears to have been overlooked by the translators of the ordinary version of the Bible in their rendering of the above-cited text from the Second Epistle of PETER. The apostle's meaning appears to have been too large for them to re-

ceive in its original simplicity of expression, and they accordingly appear, in attempting to transplant the form of his
utterance from one language into another, to have disturbed
its symmetry if not to have destroyed its vitality.

The comparison of genuine Scriptures with each other is
perhaps the readiest and most convincing mode of ascertain-
ing the limits of their value. Such comparison seems especially necessary by way of tracing discrepancies of utterance
to crudities of experience and doctrine, precision in thought
being presumably antecedent to precision in expression, even
under the guidance of inspiration. A notable instance of
such discrepancy occurs in the Mosaic narrative of GOD's
strivings with the chosen people in the establishment of the
Levitical Law, as compared with many other passages in the
sacred writings. We there find the account of what was, in
the inspired writer's apprehension, a distinct * change of purpose in the divine counsels, such as is elsewhere, with equal
distinctness, declared to be an impossibility. The great
leader, legislator and historian, appears upon that occasion
to have been hampered in his view of the divine attributes
and purposes, by the limits of his personal experience as an
agent in what may be called the merely political changes of
his day. " What will the Egyptians say?" is the query which
naturally occurred to him, as an instrument who was at the
instant but partially conscious of the magnitude of his own
mission as it has since been revealed.

It is doubtless a matter of importance that we should en-
deavor to attain clear ideas of the extent of our own capacities
and opportunities for the knowledge of the truth. There is
doubtless some fact of experience which may be justly styled
the limitation of prophecy, since man is evidently not omniscient. But we have scriptural warrant for believing that
this limitation is essentially a limitation of the power of utterance, rather than of the capacity of receiving and of the power
of retaining. It may indeed be doubted whether the human

* NUMBERS, ch. xiv.

mind is capable of conceiving any question, which it is not, in the light graciously and steadfastly vouchsafed from heaven, capable of eventually answering. The power of conception appears to be, in the ideal world, as well as in that which we more exclusively style the actual, the same with the power of production. The scriptural text which may perhaps most readily occur to the reader as seemingly opposed to this view, may be regarded as rather contributing evidence in support of it. "The secret things belong unto the LORD our God; but those things which are revealed belong unto us and to our children for ever, that we may do all the words of this law." The recipients of a twilight revelation were here assured of the permanency of their hold upon the knowledge then granted, in spite of the incompetency of its embodying language; while the suggestion of the riches of truth reserved for a more perfect administration of the Divine Power, was so vague as to claim little more than a negative value. Even then, however, the spiritual travailer for truth could doubtless anticipate the substance of the testimony of the royal Psalmist, "Thou satisfiest the desire of every living thing," and could thus attain within the restricted compass of his own thoughts, to that completeness and clearness of system which is at once the necessary concomitant of an intelligent consistency in action, the immediate object of an enlightened faith, and the sure ground of an expanding hope.

May we, who live in the days of increased and increasing illumination, not forget the dignity of our calling as intelligent beings, nor the injunction so explicitly addressed to us, that "every man be fully persuaded in his own mind!" So only may we hope as "kings and priests" unto the FATHER, to obtain grace "from Him which was, and which is, and which is to come," to interpret the words of the Law, and to know the Word of the Gospel, to the glory of GOD, and to our own assured peace.—REV. i. 6, 7, 8.

UNIVERSAL SCRIPTURE.

"In GOD we boast all the day long."—Ps. xliv. 8.

In words and in acts
　　Of human consent,
In physical facts,
　　In vigor unpent,

The universe flows,
　　A process immense
Of earnest repose
　　And gathered expense ;

While guiding its course,
　　Revealed or unknown,
Its mystical Source,
　　Sits GOD on his throne.

His heavenly rule
　　The rainbow implies,—
The chase of the fool,
　　The boast of the wise.

Thus perfectly shown,
　　Though late understood,
Be joyfully known
　　The Giver of Good !

For ever He sends
　　His edicts abroad,
In all that offends
　　And all we applaud.

His servants review
　　The line upon line,
Intent to construe
　　The writing divine.

6 *　　　　　　　　　　E

THE MORTALITY OF KNOWLEDGE.

"Whether there be knowledge, it shall vanish away."—1 Cor. xiii. 8.

THEOLOGIANS have evidently missed their mark in making a bugbear of the doctrine of Foreknowledge. Knowledge, being finite in its nature and particular in its application, is partial and contingent and therefore self-limited both in its value and duration. Wisdom is infinite and general, universal and absolute, self-developing and eternal. These cannot be empty or idle epithets, except to those to whom spiritual existence is emptiness, because of their making the material world their all in all. Knowledge is indeed the means of wisdom, as it is also the means of folly. As the staple material of every degree of intelligent intercourse, it may be called communicable wisdom, or the "wisdom of this world and of the princes of this world which cometh to naught." Knowledge, even when occurring in the form of the grandest results of the most finished culture, is essentially external, and therefore transitory. Wisdom is internal, and therefore eternal. This distinction doubtless furnishes the basis upon which we must discriminate the manifestations of mind from those of soul. How startling, how terrible, indeed, is it to the man of culture who does not constantly thus discriminate, to have to meet the announcement that knowledge must pass away! And yet how is the mortal despair which may lurk in the reflection that

"Thought lies deeper than all speech,"

extinguished in the "hope full of immortality," as he finds ability to add,

"Feeling, deeper than all thought!"

The brain is the seat of thought: the soul is the subject of experience and of independent vitality. The phenomena of consciousness and volition are most intricate, as metaphysicians might long ago, could they have anticipated the modern triumphs of mechanical invention, have *a priori* argued that they must be. That they may be counterfeited to an indefinite extent in the animal creation by the mere force of habit or instinct, especially in the more educable species, and pre-eminently in the human animal, cannot long seem to be impossible to one who considers that the contrivances of mechanics are human, while those of physiology are divine. We even profess to think and to act, often, "mechanically." Thus it is, that a custom or a notion may seem to be most firmly established by the number of its adherents, when it is upon the very brink of collapse and oblivion. In the never-ending miracle of conscious individual and social life, ideas and institutions are perishable simply because the spiritual nature in man is a progressive nature, and because progress through a world of intermingled good and evil implies a relinquishment, sooner or later, of every form of experience which is tainted with the germs of corruption. When the laws of the external life are harmonized with themselves and with those of the internal life, either in individuals or in society, progress will indeed no longer imply relinquishment, but will be an unwasting development. But until that wondrous goal shall be gained, sacrifice must be the condition of support, or formal death of essential life, even in the realm of thought and knowledge. GOD speed thee, then, honest reformer, of whatever profession, or of no profession, if thy modesty allow thee none! Go on "turning the world upside down," so far as in thee lies! The truly righteous man, who is " fully persuaded in his own mind," will not fear that his foundation shall be destroyed by thee. Foreknowledge, if it be anything, is but a form of knowledge to him. He not only knows, but he feels, that by the goodness of GOD, his temporal and eternal security is made contingent upon nothing but the just submission of his own will. His trust, and his glory, are not in institutions or in doctrines, but in GOD on high.

THE OFFENCE OF THE CROSS.

"HE hath no form nor comeliness; and when we shall see Him, there is no beauty that we should desire Him."—ISA. liii. 2.

"We preach CHRIST crucified, unto the Jews a stumbling-block, and unto the Greeks foolishness."—1 COR. i. 23.

"CHRIST hath once suffered for us, the just for the unjust, that he might bring us to GOD, being put to death in the flesh, but quickened by the SPIRIT."—1 PET. iii. 18.

THE call to perfection as sounded by the Divine Man in the Sermon on the Mount, evidently enjoins something more than the freedom from actual sin. His words were, not, Be perfect as I am perfect, but, "Be ye perfect even as your Father which is in heaven is perfect." * This language must be accepted as not only condemning all voluntary transgression, but as commanding an actual progression in the full but measurable manifestation of the divine life consequent upon obedience. As a man, the limitations of Him who "was in all points tempted like as we are, yet without sin," † were doubtless in some way more stringent than those of the subsequent generations of the race. Although "GOD gave not the Spirit by measure unto Him," ‡ He testified that his followers should "do greater works" than his, because of his going "to the FATHER." § As his own perfection in its positive aspect consisted in a progressive development of the Divine Life, so must the perfection of his faithful followers include an ever progressive triumph over inherited or acquired infirmities. As such triumph can ensue only upon a

* MATT. v. 48.   † HEB. iv. 15.   ‡ JOHN iii. 34.   § JOHN xiv. 12.

thorough spiritual conversion, the attainability of such conversion becomes plainly a most important doctrine.

Accordingly we find ourselves exhorted by the early apostles of Christianity, not so much to imitate the works of the
Saviour, as to seek the aid of his Spirit in the determination
and performance of our own. The fruits of the Spirit are
carefully commended to our cultivation, and primarily among
them that of patience or "long-suffering," as a necessary
pioneer of Christian experience. Says one, "We glory in
tribulation also, knowing that tribulation worketh patience;
and patience, experience; and experience, hope."* And
another, "The trying of your faith worketh patience; but let
patience have her perfect work, that ye may be perfect and
entire, wanting nothing."† As we read that it became the
FATHER, "for whom are all things, and by whom are all
things, in bringing many sons unto glory, to make the Captain of their salvation perfect through sufferings,"‡ so for
confirmation of our patience we are directed "to JESUS, who
for the joy that was set before Him endured the cross, despising the shame."§ Says yet another, "For even hereunto
were ye called, because CHRIST also suffered for us, leaving us
an example that ye should follow his steps."‖

As the work of spiritual progress can only be manifested
in a progressive emancipation of human life from that bondage to the corruptible forms of outward experience which is
the only possible worldly manifestation of spiritual stagna-
tion, the contest between formality and spirituality may be
said to be not only the engrossing engagement of the repentant sinner, but also the incessant labor of the militant Church,
even within its own limits. It is conceivable, it is indeed inevitably consequent upon the doctrine of perfectibility, that
spiritual and formal progress may not necessarily involve a
lifelong conflict with "the world, the flesh and the devil" on
the part of individuals; but as a whole, the Church on the

* ROM. v. 3.   † JAMES i. 4.   ‡ HEB. ii. 10.
§ HEB xii. 2.   ‖ I PET. ii. 21.

Earth is doubtless ever a Church Militant, and must expect to encounter opposition in its work of "forgetting those things which are behind, and reaching forth unto those things which are before," and so pressing toward the mark for "the prize of the high calling of God in Christ Jesus."* "As then he that was born after the flesh persecuted him that was born after the Spirit, even so it is now. . . . . If I yet preach circumcision why do I yet suffer persecution? Then is the offence of the cross ceased."† Progress, individual or collective, is manifested in the refinement of the outward forms of action and experience; but the spiritual power of the Cross is the only refining and truly vitalizing agency. That it is an offensive agency is indeed implied in its very name; but that it is eventually a harmonizing and progressive agency is implied in the doctrine of a Divine Resurrection. Successive forms of traditional propriety may and do from age to age share the fate of the obsolete observances of the Jewish ritual, supplying thus the ground of conflict and the occasion of triumph to successive generations of spiritual warriors; and the all-important strife must continue to rage and to advance until the prophesied day of consummation, of which " no man, no, not the angels which are in heaven, neither the Son, but the Father knoweth."‡ Until that eternal Sabbath shall dawn upon the Church, it must contain struggling members, who will find a labor of suffering, engrafted upon their zeal for the truth by their love for the brethren, and therefore seemingly undergone on their behalf, to be the constant condition of all their rejoicing. Surely, they may be well content to "fill up that which is left behind of the afflictions of Christ in their flesh for his body's sake, which is the Church,"§ being emboldened by faith in the resurrectional power of a spiritual crucifixion, to defy the imitative transformations of the subtle Power of Evil, although standing " in jeopardy every hour,"‖ until the complete re-

---

* Phil. iii. 13, 14.   † Gal. iv. 29; v. 11.   ‡ Mark xiii. 32; Matt. xxiv. 36.
§ Col. i. 24.   ‖ 1 Cor. xv. 30.

covery from their natural infirmity or accruing depravity shall turn all their sorrow into joy.

"Whoso is wise and will observe these things, even he shall understand the loving-kindness of the LORD." * By thus securing an interest in the "one offering" whereby the continual High Priest "hath perfected for ever all them that are sanctified," will the Christian warrior of whatever degree ever be able to conclude his remonstrances with vacillating brethren, with the confession and admonition of the catholic apostle in his epistle to the "foolish Galatians :"—"But GOD forbid that I should glory save in the cross of our LORD JESUS CHRIST, by whom the world is crucified unto me, and I unto the world. For in JESUS CHRIST neither circumcision availeth anything, nor uncircumcision, but a new creature. And as many as walk according to this rule, peace be on them and mercy, and upon the Israel of GOD. From henceforth let no man trouble me ; for I bear in my body the marks of the LORD JESUS. Brethren, the grace of our LORD JESUS CHRIST be with your spirit. Amen."

* Ps. cvii. 43.

VANITY OF VANITIES.

" If in this life only we have hope in Christ, we are of all men most miserable."—1 Cor. xv. 19.

THE force of attraction is doubly displayed:
Between subject and object it acts,—
The clasp of a fitness transcendently made
By the GOD, or the will, which attracts.

All knowledge implies but a fitness, as shown
By attraction, when conscious as love,
While subject and object in concert are known,
Through an impulse derived from above.

One world we discover within us, as one
Correspondent is opened without :
By various progress their circle is run,
As we move in assurance or doubt.

Meanwhile, whether faithful or doubting, we find,
By the inward the outward controlled,
And matter submissively carried by mind,
As by solvents, the solids they hold.

In running the round, if that inner world share
With predominance due our esteem,
Its certain completion in joy or despair
Will no meaningless mystery seem.

Not matters without us, nor motives within,
Can be heralds of GOD, to the thought
Whose course is involved in the darkness and din
Which prevail when mere objects are sought.

And joyless indeed were the Christian's career,
Could the bawbles which dazzle the sense
Of idler and worldling, supplant the pure cheer
Which enlivens his labor intense.

MERIT.

" I have seen an end of all perfection, but thy commandment is exceeding broad."—Ps. cxix. 96.

IT has been remarked by a celebrated author, as a characteristic of the unsophisticated vigor of the earnestly in-
quiring mind, that " things take the signature of thought." *
The longer we live, if we live deliberately and independently,
the more fully do we realize the fact that external nature is
but a mirror upon which are shadowed in demonstrable out-
lines of beauty or deformity, the principles of our interior experience.   To assert this, even in anticipation of the realization, would be but to extend to our human nature, the
observation which we all find to be true in subordinate
spheres of knowledge, that force is ever interior to form.
In both cases is the force, or life, concealed by the form, or
body, and yet revealed by it.   Indeed it may be said to be
concealed by it in order that it may be revealed by it, as the
ordained channel for the communication of intelligence.   It
is thus that the material world may be said to confess itself
the servant of the spiritual, ever closely following and legibly
registering its progress in the harmony and power of truth.

Never, indeed, without conflict, is the supremacy of the
ideal over the actual experimentally maintained.   The spiritual domain of emotions and motives must witness a triumph
within itself over the intrusive suggestions of sloth and dis-
cord, before it can manifest itself in efficient and harmonious
action.   Only by perseverance in the uncompromising war-

. * COLERIDGE.

74

fare which the Son of God, and Saviour of men, descended from Heaven to institute, and lives in Heaven to direct, are the eternal freshness and power of truth to be realized in inward and outward fruits of happiness and peace and glory. The life of the faithful Christian, and it alone, is endowed with the subtle graces and genuine activity of perennial youth.

Youth itself, however, may be said to be a form, as well as a force. As a phenomenon of time and space, it bears precedence among the controlling conditions of every individual existence. Through the neglect of its spiritual potentialities it may become a decaying and corrupt form ; but as it is animated by the love of truth and duty, it is found to be at once firmly conservative and irresistibly progressive. By the exercise of the Divine charity which believes, hopes, and endures all things, while it may seemingly ignore the existence of essential evil, it grasps and wields the only weapons which can oppose and overcome it. Steadfastly ceasing to do evil in its own preconceived forms of work, it as steadfastly learns to do well in the life of faith ; and its path is " as a shining light, shining more and more unto the perfect day." The perfection of yesterday may become the imperfection of to-day ; but the "exceeding broad commandment" remains to conduct it onward to the perfect manhood of " the measure of the stature of the fullness of Christ."

It is perhaps one of the least imperfect or improper, and therefore one of the most persistent and most useful illusions of the youthful pilgrim, to place more or less confidence in the fallible authority of his fellow-man. The prescription of tradition, and the prestige of service, seem to him to invest merely occasional rules and merely mortal examples, with the sanction of universal and enduring applicability. By them he is willing to be guided, and to them he would fain appeal " that his deeds may be made manifest that they are wrought in God." For only as the education of nature is entirely subordinated to that of grace, is the promised sonship attained, whose happiness it is to distinguish the one immediate, undeceitful and Divine Light, from all transmitted or reflected radiance. But so far as the standard and the sanction of the Christian neophyte may be thus in the keeping of his fellow-man, he cannot "be fully persuaded in his own mind," and his store of rejoicing must be accordingly not in himself, but "in another." The depth and fullness of the promise, "when my father and my mother forsake me, then the LORD will take me up," must remain to be realized by him. One by one his mortal authorities must fail to fulfil his purest expectations, as they more or less gradually expose their own natural limitations; while still others will be at hand to attract the allegiance of his imperfect faith, until the revelation of righteousness in the gospel "from faith to faith" shall finally emancipate him from all dependence upon mortal priesthoods. Then will he first fully realize with regard to his fellows, that which he may perhaps long before have discovered with regard to himself, that whatever merit there may be in human works, there is none in the human worker; but in Him who shall have wrought all their works in them. ISA. xxvi. 12.

THE SUBORDINATION OF LAW.

"EVERY man in his own order."—1 COR. xv. 23.

IT being the object of Law to define duty rather than privilege,—the right of work rather than the right of enjoyment,—they who seek through it for privilege or enjoyment are apt to find themselves grievously disappointed. It is only secondarily, or by being primarily the surety of work, that Law is ever the surety of enjoyment. The law of labor can nevertheless become the law of happiness to those who order their desires in accordance with the terse and trite proverb, "Business first, and pleasure afterward." "Blessed," exclaims an indefatigable though variously appreciated teacher,* "is the man who has found his work!" The intelligent and faithful workman is indeed a freeman, and a sovereign in his sphere.

As there are, however, different spheres of labor, so there are different spheres of Law; the superior in either case, by virtue of the unity and consistency of all truth, comprehending the inferior to the extent in which they may be associated. The law of the subject is thus identical, so far as it may reach with that of the ruler, and can only gain in efficiency and interest by approximating to it. The suggestions of a true superior to a faithful inferior can therefore never be intrusive or annoying; but being a part of the communion of love, they will, like every other form of genuine charity, be elevating and enlarging to both "him who gives and him who takes." The same power of love, which can alone, as the law of labor, perfectly "cast out fear" in ourselves, may also, as the law of happiness, exclude hostility in others, and thus become

* THOMAS CARLYLE.

both privately and publicly the law of prosperity and of peace. Subordination is thus simply one of the elements of harmony. Step by step must the naturally dependent and short-sighted worker rise to the discovery that " he that dwelleth in love dwelleth in GOD, and GOD in him," realizing therein only the fulfilment of the divine injunction, "Whosoever will be chief among you, let him be your servant."

AUTHORITY.

" In that day shall there be one LORD, and his name One."—ZECH. xiv. 9.

THOU wouldst not lose thy dignity !—Well said.
If so thou meanest humbly to confess
Thy own subjection to the mighty Head,
Whose will each member must in acts express.

But art thou yet indeed his member ?   Hast
Thou naught of joy in any life, except
In that clear stream with which his Oneness vast
From kindred veins each selfish taint hath swept ?

Authority, where decently maintained,
Must flow in living order.   Stagnate not
By resting in the posture thou hast gained,
Dreaming thyself creation's central spot.

Forsake thyself : reject the bonds of sense :
O'er time and space, seek with thy spirit's eye
An Essence vaster than their vague immense,
And find within thyself the Eternal Why !

Within thee, though not of thee, GOD shall then
Extend his throne, and share with thee his rule
O'er all his works, and o'er unholy men,
To curb the headstrong, and reprove the fool.

Subordination then will be thy aim,
First for thyself, and then for those around,
That each thereby may press his humble claim
For strength and joy, where both are fully found.

All nature, then, true to the primal law
Of order, shall show forth its Sovereign's will,
While gently tempering his o'erpowering awe
Through his vicegerents widely working still.

ABSTRACTIONS *versus* DELUSIONS.

"For the time will come when they will not endure sound doctrine."—
2 TIM. iv. 3, 4.

THERE is what may be called a divine music in a well-
ordered life. The genuine intelligence and ample comprehension which belong to the divine nature in the renewed
man, express themselves necessarily and yet freely, to those
who have "ears to hear," in the language of an unbroken
harmony. All things being "done decently and in order"
no true interest is neglected, and none is pursued in an improper time, place, or mode. Such a life will be likely to
appear monotonous if not unmeaning to observers whose
habits of thought are dislocated from its happy integrity by
an undue devotion to any of the subordinate interests which
enter into the composition of its one leading interest, because
to such the main objects of their life will seem to be recognized only to be set at naught. They will see that everything
which is necessary for the existence of their idols is preserved,
while the idols themselves will appear to be overlooked from
the mere fact of their being in turn subordinated to the preser-
vation of the still larger interest or interests, which ever lie beyond the reach of an imperfect faith. Truth, which is the greatest reality, is also the greatest abstraction ; and there is always
a point at which the pursuit of it for its own sake, must appear
but as weariness and foolishness to all whose vision is either
lost in the mists of a groveling sensuality, or diverted from
the Central Luminary by the gilded clouds of a more refined
and aspiring selfishness. While this is their condition, how

can they do otherwise than "despise the voice of the charmer, charming never so wisely?"

Every definable rule of life may be called an abstraction, and must become a delusive one as it is made to usurp the place of the indefinable and only universal rule of the Divine Spirit of life and truth. This only can enable us in all cases to observe the Divine precept, "Judge not according to the appearance, but judge righteous judgment." Every motive which may seem to ourselves to begin or end in any definite object of created good, is but "vanity" and must land us in "vexation of spirit." The only remunerative service is the service of the bountiful Creator, and this is at all times incompatible with a primary pursuit of worldly attainment. "Ye cannot serve GOD and Mammon." Money, which is the most universally recognized representative of worldly good, thus becomes the most delusive of abstractions, as it is mentally abstracted or detached from its place in the divine order of truth, and elevated from the rank of a means to that of an end. Here, at least, experience is found to agree with theory. The late STEPHEN GIRARD, whose success in accumulating money was of course no proof that he was at heart a worshiper of Mammon, however his mind may have lacked the development which a timely discipline of nobler rules might have ensured, avowed at the very zenith of his seeming prosperity, that his main object in life was to work hard enough in the day-time to be able to sleep soundly at night. According as his success was a substantial or an empty one, how must he have smiled, either in pity or in scorn, upon the multitudes whom he beheld around him eagerly enlisted in the pursuit of his glittering abstraction !

Position, popularity, reputation, praise, and immortality, are names by which "the world" recognizes different degrees of its other favorite abstraction. These also, so far as they are realities, are but variously imposing and fleeting forms of the Power which consists solely in the knowledge and love of the truth. As they are attained in the spirit of insubordination to the truth, they too must prove to be but delusive phantoms, and the unhappy aspirant will ever be constrained mentally to repeat the melancholy demand, " Is this all?"

" The concrete" is in some sense the opposite of " the abstract." By the one epithet we mean an embodied or communicable good or evil ; and by the other, a disembodied or incommunicable. The rule of self-denying love, which is the law of liberty, is also that of all true realization and communication. By it only, as revealed through faith in the Divine Son by the Holy Spirit can we realize the strength which is to be found in union with one another, and in communion with the Father of spirits. The only way to avoid the delusions and disappointments of the scattering voices of " Lo! here," and " Lo ! there," is thus to seek the kingdom which is only to be found within us. This pursuit will involve a willing abstraction from all dependence upon sensual and artificial aids, but it will be a triumphant abstraction, whose victory will be qualified by no mixture of unhappy disappointment. " The concrete" may indeed be said to mean the whole of life, but the promise of the blessed Saviour remains in force, " He that loses his life for my sake and the gospel's shall find it."

Only as we begin our pilgrim course with this holy abstraction, can we hope to avoid by the way those which are unholy and delusive, and to close our struggles with the exulting exclamation, " the half has not been told." Only as we thus bring all our crowns to the foot of the cross of Christ the Saviour, can we hope to join the throng of those who even now come " from the uttermost parts of the earth " to behold the glory of Him who is " greater than Solomon !"

HIDDEN LIFE.

"THE grave cannot praise Thee, death cannot celebrate Thee: they that go down into the pit cannot hope for thy truth.

"The living, the living, he shall praise Thee, as I do this day: the father to the son shall make known thy truth."—ISA. xxxviii. 18, 19.

FAITH in doctrine,* hope for truth,† and love to GOD,‡ may be styled the successive stages of a religious life. Each of these stages, after the first, being essentially a confirmation and extension rather than an abandonment of that which has preceded it, the aspiration of such a life is for growth or development, rather than for any externally prescribed attainment, which might be at the best but a rambling appearance of gain. Owing to the variety of present circumstances and previous opportunities in different individuals, the manifestations of these different stages may be often alike, or indistinguishable from each other by any prescribed rule, so that no definite standard of spiritual vitality can be safely assumed. The "fruits of the Spirit" must indeed be sooner or later recognizable, either in their increase or in their decrease, to the spiritually minded observer, whose eye is single and whose "whole body" is accordingly "full of light;" so that such an one may be divinely enabled to see the direction in which the feet of his fellow-man are moving:

* "Faith cometh by hearing, and hearing by the Word of GOD."—ROM. x. 17.

† "We are saved by hope: but hope that is seen is not hope."—ROM. viii. 24.

‡ "GOD is love: and he that dwelleth in love dwelleth in GOD, and GOD in him."—1 JOHN iv. 16.

yet even such an one is for the most part happily exempted from the necessity of deciding how nearly the steps of a companion have reached, on the one hand, to the goal of perfect devotion, or on the other to the limit of the Divine toleration and mercy, and of distinguishing the precise period at which his face may begin to turn from the course which he has been pursuing. We may even be " living in pleasures," and there. fore " dead while we live," and the dreadful reality may, in very mercy, be indiscernible to those who love and care for us, that our religion is an empty form, our faith that of the devils who " believe and tremble," and our whole life a state of spiritual bondage, under whatever disguise of seeming freedom and happiness.

The grave is the hopeless home of corruption to all who do not spiritually descend into its inevitable gulf by faith in Him who overcame death. So far as any have experienced the power and submitted to the dominion of sin, they must be made " dead with CHRIST," before they can also live with Him. The outward interment and decay of our corruptible bodies is not more fitly symbolical of the spiritual condition of those who reject the terms of heavenly grace, than the temporary repose of the mortal part of the holy Captain of salvation in its rock-hewn sepulchre may symbolize the temporary or apparent withdrawal from wonted scenes of action, of lives which are undergoing the all-important conversion from the state of nature to the state of grace. The strength of these may be as completely veiled from the view of their fellow-mortals, as is the weakness of their benighted contemporaries ; and they may appear by comparison as ghastly spectres, walking the Earth but to destroy the pleasant pictures of GOD's creation. Already, nevertheless, such are practical preachers of the " baptism of repentance," and heralds, to those who have hearts to understand, of the solemn decree, that the " fashion of this world" shall pass away. As they keep the word of Divine patience, the promised day of redemption from the power of temptation will follow. Their Saviour will "come quickly," and the crown which no man shall take away will be their reward. Only such can ever be entitled and prepared to respond to the animating summons, "Arise, shine: for thy light is come, and the glory of the LORD is risen upon thee. For behold, the darkness shall cover the earth, and gross darkness the people : but the LORD shall arise upon thee, and his glory shall be seen upon thee." * For of them that sleep in the dust of the earth, some shall awake "to everlasting life, and some to shame and everlasting contempt." "But they that be wise shall shine as the brightness of the firmament, and they that turn many to righteousness as the stars for ever and ever." †

* Isa. lx. 1, 2.   † Dan. xii. 2, 3.

8

A PARAPHRASE.

Ps. cxxx.

OUT of the depths we cry to Thee ;
Hear Thou our voice attentively !
O LORD ! with all our dreams of merit,
What wealth can willful works inherit?

Forgiveness is the boon we seek,
Before the blessing of the meek.
Let mercy's gates expand before us ;
Then as we run, do Thou restore us.

Our startling fear, our steadfast hope,
What scheming with thy Word can cope?
For Thee we wait and thy adorning,
Like watchers wishing for the morning.

More eagerly than these we pray,
Spread in our hearts thine endless day,
As, through the scenes of thy creation,
Each soul evolves its own salvation.   [Phil. ii. 12.]

Thy called and chosen each shall be,
Who struggles in sincerity,
To conquer every inbred giant
Which mocks thy rule with deeds defiant.

Like ISRAEL, then, may we prevail,
As one man, o'er our common ail ;
And, shielded by thy Son's exemption,
Attain thy plenteous redemption !

Thy kingdom come, thy will be done,
While thus our earthly race we run :
And o'er each good Thou still suppliest,
Sing we thy glory in the highest !
　4th Mo., 1863.

A POSSIBLE STEP FORWARD.

" WHERE is the promise of his coming ?"—2 PET. iii. 4.

[NOTE.—It may be due to the reader to state that this piece was designed as a substantial reproduction of the first few pages of that on CONVERSATION AND EDUCATION, which shortly follows. It was written wholly at the suggestion of a valued counselor, who thought the matter might be thrown into a more popular form, for a philanthropic periodical just then, as it turned out, on the eve of discontinuance.]

" THE desire of a man is his kindness," said the wise king. Necessary as it is to preach the gospel of good works by way of shutting out bad works in our age and country of physical energy and material abundance, we cannot yet afford to lose sight of the principle that it is the spirit of the doer which mainly qualifies the deed. The great circle of practical truth may be equally broken, and the work of practical religion equally interrupted, by a misanthropic listlessness, and by the merely formal or imitative activity which may equally coexist with an actual sluggishness of spirit.

But while all earnest workers must be at times painfully conscious of this tendency to superficiality and consequent futility in our best life, we seem to have been as yet much at a loss for the means of expressing our condition and of so being prepared intelligently and unitedly to shun its dangers. It is naturally difficult for any of us,—and the difficulty may be only confirmed by association with those of like antecedents and surroundings with ourselves,—to realize that the most seemingly definite knowledge is modified by the extent and

87

form of our individual capacity, or that every item of truth has universal relations by virtue of which it is capable of expanding with our expanding capacities. Knowledge is a progressive, because a relative, thing. While Truth is immortal, " Knowledge," we are divinely assured, " shall vanish away." Knowledge consists in the conscious adaptation of our present selves or senses to our present circumstances, or in other words, in the relation of a "subjective" or internal element to an " objective" or external element, and is necessarily as transient or mutable as either of the elements upon which it depends. In these qualities of all merely human knowledge, we may trace the original necessity of the mysterious bond of individual faith (Rom. xiv. 22) as the only hope of consistency, and the reason of the subsequent supremacy of the rule of individual experience. Rom. xiv. 5.

The distinction between subjective and objective truth being a primary condition of all human consciousness, is therefore also a primary consideration in the just estimation of human motives. These terms " objective" and " subjective" have been too long the exclusive property of metaphysicians, and, as might have been anticipated, the metaphysicians have to some extent abused their monopoly. They have too much failed to teach the transitory value of thought as an object of endowment, and the still more transitory value of language, as a still more superficial object. The so-called " Philosophy of Common Sense" of REID and HAMILTON, now widely prevailing, may be styled a systematic repudiation of the objectivity of Thought. Maintaining that external things are themselves the real objects of original Perception, and thus implying that we see everything that we see at all exactly as it is, it so far removes all inducement to correcting our perceptions and extending our insight by the processes of comparison and analysis. We need not inquire whether it professes to do so, since error is ever inconsistent. By failing justly to distinguish between thoughts and things as objects alike, though in different degrees or distances, external to the thinker, it admits if it does not advocate a repeal of every principle of progress. *Crescit eundo,* " it grows with going," is a law which is especially applicable to the march of mind, but no scope is allowed for its operation here. Old forms of thought perish by being absorbed and transformed into larger and fairer ones, which they could not be, were our perceptions originally of things as they truly are.

There is a constant revolution in the progress of mind, and it may be that that revolution and progress cannot be understood without a regard to the principle of Polarity. It would seem that there are subjective and objective poles and hemispheres of experience or knowledge, just as there are the North and South poles of the globe we outwardly tread. Scriptural testimony is not wanting as to the fact and mode of the continual growth of mind. It must clearly be by reason of such growth rather than of any selfish or studied reserve, that the " wise man" keeping his thought " till afterward" is presented as having an advantage over " the fool" who " utters all his mind ;" and this because his sufficiency is not of himself, his supplies being all drawn from a Source which is confessedly incomprehensible to himself. In the more explicit though more comprehensive language of the New Testament, " the righteousness of GOD is revealed from faith to faith ;" and is not the philosophy of polarity poetically recognized in that of the Psalmist, " Beautiful for situation, the joy of the whole earth, is Mount Zion on the sides of the North ;" and again, " Promotion cometh neither from the East, nor from the West, nor from the South"?

Purity and peace are primary characteristics (JAMES iii. 17) of the "Wisdom which is from above." I would say nothing to degrade them either as subjects or as objects from their scriptural eminence among the Christian graces. I have only to urge that they should be pursued as being indeed qualities of the Wisdom which is from above, in which case there will be no danger of their being detached from other virtues. With this view we assuredly need to study the laws of

8 *

thought in their necessary connection with the laws of action as important means of preserving us from superficial activities, or so-called hobby-riding. Where the love of display, which is so apt to attend the pursuit of any definitely prescribed effect, to any extent supplants the disinterested guidance of individual faith, spiritual intelligence must be proportionally dormant, and religion at best retrograde from the freedom of the gospel to the bondage of the law. There must sooner or later be a subversion of the true motives of thought and action, the unknown being subordinated to the known, or aspiration to attainment; and the comparatively trifling mysteries of the latest witchcraft will so far obscure and obstruct the miraculous growth and triumph of Christian truth. One of the broadest injunctions of Holy Writ is that of him who may be called the analytical apostle, " Let all things be done decently and in order ;" and it seems to me that one of our next steps forward must be a more general recognition of the just subordination of the Objective to the Subjective, of the phenomenal to the real, of the past to the coming, of the passing to the lasting, which is traceable through all degrees of progress in knowledge. Let us remember that all the efforts of skepticism have failed to disprove that there is a real and lasting Power of Evil, to which we may by carelessness in any direction become victims.

INCIDENTAL EDUCATION.

"I WILL bring the blind by a way that they knew not."—ISA. xliii. 16.

EDUCATION, like every other special business or experience, may be either direct or indirect. As the influence of the teacher may be either designed or undesigned on
his part, so the progress of the learner may be either conscious or unconscious on his. By indirect or incidental education, I mean the progress which while unconscious on the
part of the pupil, is not undesigned on that of the tutor. By
virtue of the fact of his having been before over the ground
which they are traversing together, the intelligent tutor is able
in the realm of his own consciousness to be at once before
and behind his junior companion, while seeming perhaps to
be only at his side. It is his business to know not only the
work which is to be done, but also the character and circumstance of the worker, in some respects at least, better than
they are known to himself, so that speaking as it were from
behind him, or from the direction in which he is least
known to himself, he may be able to check every deviation
with the cry, "this is the way, walk in it."

I do not mean to claim for the teacher the prerogative of
priesthood beyond the necessity of his calling; but it seems
clear to me that to a certain extent he must, if he teach anything thoroughly, realize and illustrate the doctrine that faith
must precede mental and spiritual vision. So far as the
pupil may need to be supplied through human channels
with the inspiration which shall impel him to make use of

his opportunities, I would say that it is the teacher's business intelligibly to point the precept, "Know the LORD." This, I conceive he will surely do by a faithful adherence to the rule that the development of hidden principles is incidental to the teaching of obvious facts.

The direct teaching of facts or objects is conscious learning to the pupil, because it consists in a definite addition to his fund of knowledge. The incidental development of principles is indirect teaching and unconscious learning, because it seems at first to be nothing more than the orderly arrangement of knowledge. As the learner, however, becomes familiar with this orderly arrangement of knowledge, the principles of harmony and unity on which it depends become recognized by him as being themselves the most substantial of facts. Although at a previous stage of his progress he might have spurned their announcement as the preaching of mere abstractions or purely subjective notions, he now values them as being in his own experience the most permanent of realities. Thus he is qualified to act in his turn the part of an intelligent truth-teacher to those who may still be in bondage to the beggarly elements of a comparatively superficial life and knowledge.

The science of language, being a metaphysical science, is of course one in which we cannot look for such an early appreciation of principles as in the mathematical and more obviously physical departments of knowledge. In all alike a hint may be taken from the recipe of the facetious *cuisinier*, "first catch the fish." The "raw material" is of course, in all, the basis not only of observation, but of communication. To the pupil, at least, the teacher ought always to be wiser than his books,—the virtual embodiment of the truth which they profess to illustrate. In contemplating language as the vehicle, and thought as the material of education, let us remember that while the science of language is practically inseparable from the science of thought, it is truly subordinate to it; and let us accordingly be prepared to inculcate, at the

very outset, the view that thoughts or ideas do not lose their
rank as things or objects, merely by being reduced, and as it
were refined, into a concentrated form of experience, so that
they can be carried in the memory along with their associated words. There may be a transient mysticism in such
teaching, but even this may be regarded as an incidental
advantage in a doctrine so fundamentally important. Even
children cannot too early realize the truth that knowledge in
the distance is necessarily mystical, nor be too early guarded
against confounding mysticism with absurdity. Their interest will be more likely to be stimulated than checked by this
simple, straightforward policy, not only in the study of language, but in that of every other science which can be made
the subject of language. By their unsophisticated instru-
mentality, let us doubt not, even teachers may be incidentally
aided in developing the order of wisdom out of our chaos of
knowledge, so that the world will again be able to accept and
careful to cherish the now discarded maxim, *Scientiarum
janitrix grammatica*, Grammar is the janitress of the
sciences.

KNOWLEDGE.

"Add to knowledge temperance."—2 Pet. i. 6.

The knowledge which answers a need,
  Is that which wise learners will love:
Where our nature is wanting indeed,
  May its increase be sought from above!

For who of us fathoms his wants?
  Who sees through the crowd of his cares,
And, in fairest or gloomiest haunts,
  To meet each in its order prepares?

Man's cravings, of hunger and thirst,
  For action, and thought, and repose,
In their freshness rank each as the first,
  And of each, by its objects, he knows.

Such knowledge avails him not long:
  In physical concert it stands,
And ensures not the nutriment strong
  Which the flight of the spirit demands.

That nutriment still, as a child,
  Truth's earnest explorer shall find,
And with knowledge imbibe, unbeguiled
  By the adjuncts of matter or mind.

So reaching from every height
  The knowledge in feeling begun,
Will he soon in the verdict unite,
  —There is no new thing under the sun.*

But gaining by staff and by rod
  The comfort which all things augment,
He will know of the only true God,
  And of Jesus, the Christ He hath sent†

* Eccles. i. 9.   † John xvii. 2.

THE EXPENDITURE OF EXPLANATION.

"From the fact that they had Reason in abundance, they were somewhat chary of reasons. Their thinking, indeed, gives us the solid, nutritious, enriching substance of Thought, ... and especially avoids the thinness and juicelessness which are apt to characterize the greatest efforts of the understanding, when understanding is divorced from character."—E. P. WHIPPLE, *on the Thinkers of the Age of* ELIZABETH.

IN the Scriptures of the New Testament, besides the general commendations of the spirit of unsuspecting charity on the part of all men toward their fellow-beings, we find particular occasions or modes mentioned for its exercise. We are distinctly exhorted to give alms of our material and intellectual substance as well as of our spiritual sympathy, with the view, doubtless, of leading us to realize in ourselves the riches of the true spiritual charity, which cannot be maintained and demonstrated without such outward communication. He who shall petition us for a reason of "the hope that is in us," as well as he who shall come to us for the relief of his bodily necessities, if we can believe that he is making his request with a single view to qualifying himself for the discharge of his duties in the Divine sight, is to be treated by us as one of "GOD'S poor" whose claims upon our attention are incontrovertible and imperative. By the neglect of such we lose the opportunity of laying up "treasure in Heaven." This is indeed a consideration of primary and permanent importance to all who may find themselves to be in any degree the stewards of any kind of influence over their fellow-men.

There is, however, another, and an opposite danger which besets all professors of religion, in proportion as they may be remiss in the ever urgent duty of scrutinizing their own motives and rules of action. The vice of officiousness is sure to overtake those in whom slothfulness of spirit has induced a reliance upon the mere letter of religion. Both the nature of their own emotions, and the characteristic circumstances of those with whom they have to deal, will be sure to be misinterpreted by such, and there must be a correspondingly ignorant misapplication and practical waste of their labor and means. The evils of material thriftlessness which may be thus harbored, and even fostered to the magnitude of oppressive social burdens, are comparatively well known in our day. The danger of fostering a permanent system of intellectual pauperism seems to be less generally deprecated, as being less superficial, and therefore at once less obviously disgraceful to its victims, and more secretly seductive to those who may find in it a source of factitious influence. Its mischievous results must doubtless, however, be more extensive, in proportion as its origin and operation are more insidious. "Man that is in honor, and understandeth not, is like the brutes that perish."

The application of the divine precept, "Give not that which is holy unto the dogs, neither cast ye your pearls before swine," must be to some extent obvious to almost all. The great difficulty here, as in the observance of every literal precept of social duty, is that of remembering upon all occasions that our own impressions of character may be at fault, even where they appear to be most distinct. If, when compelled by the conduct of our fellow-beings, according to our best interpretation of it, to treat them as insensible beings, we are careful to bear in mind that our interpretation may nevertheless be deficient, the harshness of our demeanor will not be aggravated by the spirit of arrogance. Whether, then, the discipline which we have to administer be that of neglect or that of attention, its outlay must evidently, by the avoid ance of futile exasperation, be economically adapted to any remaining sensibility of the recipient. The sources of healthful feeling, which are the sources of accuracy in thought as well as of harmony in action, will thus be as effectually reached and stimulated as they can be by human agency.

As the work of education in both young and old consists in the development of the power of independent observation and reflection, so the labor of explanation may be said ever to resolve itself into one of mere suggestion. Dictation, in matters of opinion, ever implies officiousness, or the zeal which is " not according to knowledge," if it do not proceed from outright hostility. As the constitution of human society approaches the ideal of perfection, the old and serviceable trinity, of duty, power and privilege, must still determine the degrees of worldly rank ; but in the administration of an enlightened charity, the duty, the power and the privilege, must be increasingly manifested, as to their merely social bearings, in the mere labor of making suggestions. Not the less, however, will the continual fruitfulness of all feeling, thought, and expression, depend upon the spiritual vigilance which shows itself equally in the anticipation of all genuine demands upon its resources, and in the avoidance of all officious wastefulness. "Wisdom is profitable to direct."* "Wisdom is justified of her children." † "In thy light shall we see light." ‡

* Eccles. x. 10.   † Matt. xi. 19.   ‡ Ps. xxxvi. 9.

CONVERSATION AND EDUCATION.

"LET the word of CHRIST dwell in you richly in all wisdom, teaching and admonishing one another."—COL. iii. 16.

START not, O gentle reader! and frown not, O strong-minded! at any seeming incongruity in the terms of our title. Even among those to whom we may seem to be confounding beginning with ending, opin-

Unity and scope of the subject. ions may differ as to which is the beginning and which the ending; and is it not always worthy of commemoration that extremes of experience, save as contingent upon extravagancies of conduct, are secretly and harmoniously correlated? Even Etymology indicates that the most contrasted objective terms are, or express, but opposite *termini* of practical truth; and Cosmography assures us that the North and South Poles are but a sort of Siamese Twins. Let us see if we cannot so identify the world of Education with that of Conversation, as to give to both of those terms a vitality and an interest which we too often fail to find in the imperfect abstractions or the capricious developments which they are made to represent.

(1.) A view from within. First, as to motives. In both we have at first to deal with the comparatively super-ficial love of man and the dependent desire for human appro-bation, rather than with the deeper-seated love of GOD and the more independent aspiration for abstract truth; while in both, with the development or manifestation of independence of character, the labor of exhortation and dictation will be replaced by that of intelligent demonstration and candid in-

quiry, as becomes the possessors of an illumination by which all distinctions of personality are thrown into the shade. Alike in Science and in Religion personal authority must give way to that of argument and of a dividual experience, as the neophyte is graduated into the proficient. Abstractly, this consideration may seem almost too simple and obvious to demand mention ; but in practice it must be acknowledged that it is very often lost sight of, owing to the imperfection of prevailing theories inducing imperfection of practice. One of these imperfections we may now pause to contemplate.

Thought is superior to language. But it becomes practically inferior in the experience of any who have not learned, or who do not bear in mind, that they are indeed two distinct things. Speech being but the means of our meaning, the mere vehicle of the treasures of mind, should never be pursued or paraded as an end. When we speak, we should speak as those who are trying to be silent ; and not, even when silent, be silent as those whose powers are consumed by the desire to speak. We have too much lost the meaning of the sacred proverb, "A fool uttereth all his mind, but a wise man keepeth it in till afterward." It is only by a continual comparison of our words with our meaning, that we can assure ourselves that we are indeed willing to be still, and possessing our souls in patience, while giving vent to our feelings in speech. This consideration brings to our view a more general principle, of which the distinction between thought and speech is but a single aspect or illustration ; namely, that primary condition of all human consciousness, the distinction between subjective and objective truth. These terms have heretofore been too exclusively the property of the metaphysician. The common mind seems now preparing to assert its right to their use, and to profit by the observation that Thought relatively to Language is Subjective, and Language relatively to Thought, Objective.

Hidden errors, and the hidden clue of truth.

The whole mystery of these terms lies in their relativity. Thought, although subjective in its relation to language, is, in accordance with a more or less prevailing sentiment among investigators in all ages until our own, objective in its relation to the Thinker. It is the bane of modern Philosophy, as represented by the now dominant school of REID and HAMILTON, that it fails to recognize the distinct existence of ideas as the immediate objects both of reflective Consciousness and of direct Perception. The assumed alternative, that external things are the immediate objects of Perception, is essentially absurd and suicidal, since it plainly involves the assumption that the mind, or percipient subject, is in direct contact with things as they are, and the inevitable inference that we perceive more than we either understand or remember, and are in fact unconsciously omniscient. There are indeed the abstract ideas, which, as the objects of Memory and the materials of Imagination, are distinguishable from the concrete ideas of actual Perception, and which by reason of their prior incorporation with the mind may be termed subjective, relatively to those which are the immediate results of present Perception. But this subjectivity is simply identical with that of all Thought to all Language, the materials of language being, as is now conclusively established, wholly supplied by those external impressions in which all men most unmistakably agree, and subsequently subjectively refined *pari passu* (even-paced) with the refinement of Thought. It extends no farther, because a healthy Memory and Imagination follow so closely in the wake of Vision, that there can be no practical discrimination between their objects for individual purposes. As a rule, old ideas become continually in themselves more objective and obsolete, and seem to retain their subjective vitality only by the continued development of mind resulting from continued observations upon life and nature, and the retention of old terms of language in correspondingly extended significations. "Whether there be knowledge, it shall vanish away." The universal subordination of the Objective to the

Subjective, including that of parts to wholes, and indirectly at least that of individuals to communities, is the only intelligible clue of approach toward the perfection in which all " that which is in part shall be done away."

The independence of Thought upon Lan- The precedence guage being thus, as it were, a constituent part of thought. of healthy, human character, must be cherished as a leading motive in every worthy labor both of language and of thought, and so become a most important bond of union and law of relationship between the great and greatly unknown provinces of human Conversation and human Education. Let us now turn more particularly to an examination of the materials which are common to both.

Here again we are met by the relativity and (2.) seemingly merely verbal nature of intellectual External aspects. distinctions, the consideration of first and final causes of actions being inseparable from any earnest consideration of their nature and value. We cannot, that is, pretend to draw a fixed line here between motives and materials; but by making due allowance for the subordination and inherent imbecility of language as the mere tool of thought, we shall doubtless be enabled to proceed both more intelligently and more hopefully than they who cripple their own minds by secretly imputing to Thought the limitations of Language.

For the proper materials both of Conversa- tion and of Education we must doubtless look The distinction a relative one, de- without ourselves, as for the motives of both pending on the men- we have had to look within ourselves. The tal position of the inquirer. progressive enlargement of the internal realm by the progressive subjection of the external, inevitably occasions a verbal and objective confusion of those realms, where self-knowledge or wisdom does not keep pace with the knowledge of things; but the subordination of the objective to the subjective is here also the sufficient law of order, as well as of illimitable progress. That knowledge of external things which may be already at any time attained by any, is definite

9 *

and objective as compared with that which is as yet unattained, and therefore as yet, in its unknown relation to the same explorer, purely mystical and subjective. Objects of aspiration in some being often objects of attainment in others, the utility both of Conversation and of Education thus of course lies largely in the fact that our shortest road to the unknown truths even of external nature is often through the minds of other people. Hence it may well be questioned whether the study of Thought in its objective aspects has ever received that place of primary importance in the work of Education and in the display of Conversation which rightly belongs to it. An objective Science of Mind is plainly one of the indispensable materials of both, if perfection, or even if progress, be possible in either.

As regards the purely external world the distinction between subjective and objective truth may be defined as identical with that between substance and quality. Here we again discover the subtle and shifting trait of relativity,—the substance, (*quod stat subter,* as COLERIDGE writes,) ever retiring from Perception into the realm of Imagination, behind the new qualities which it successively gives off as it were to the investigating mind. The materials both of Conversation and of Education must clearly be for the most part, as regards the external world, derivative rather than immediate, or essentially intellectual rather than sensational. The laws of Mind are from first to last our chief guides and standards for classifying and estimating the said materials. Those materials are thus broadly and simply divisible into objects of Introspection and objects of Perception ; the law of relativity, as already intimated, being our safeguard from confusion, by allotting to the definite and demonstrable educts of thought which most largely influence practice, the rank of objective perceptions, while reserving that of subjective imaginations for the more vague but hopeful impressions which govern theory. Who can fail to see in these contrasting and yet co-operating elements of Mind,—

Typified by sex.

the one deriving its inspiration from within and the other
from without—a true sexual relationship, for which it may
be the highest temporal significance of sex corporeal to serve
as a symbol? It is certain that the law of mental increase is
often strangely overlooked in the contemplation of its results.
Said Dr. JOHNSON in his appreciating biography of the accomplished and indefatigable JOHN DRYDEN, " A writer who has
attained his full purpose loses himself in his own lustre.
Of an opinion which is no longer doubted, the evidence
ceases to be examined. Of an art universally practiced, the
first teacher is forgotten. Learning once made popular is no
longer learning ; it has the appearance of something which
we have bestowed upon ourselves, as the dew appears to
rise from the field which it refreshes. To judge rightly of
an author we must transport ourselves to his time, and examine what were the wants of his contemporaries and what
were his means of supplying them. That which is easy at
one time was difficult at another."* The light of inspiration
becomes inappreciable alike behind us and before us, where
attainment is not constantly combined with and subordinated
to aspiration.

The duality of mind at the contemplation
of which we thus arrive, is perhaps sufficiently represented for most occasions by the
distinction between abstract and concrete ideas ; the abstract
being ever the leaders in the common progress, and leaving
to the concrete the function of expression. The first Rule of
Arithmetic, for instance, is Addition, (not Numeration, which,
as its etymology indicates, is more justly to be regarded as a
synonym for the whole science) which deals wholly in concrete numbers. When, in the labor of adding or numerating,
we reach the number Ten, we cannot proceed farther, according to the received system of notation, without introducing the
Rule of Multiplication, in which, as is well understood, an

The subordination of mind.

* Similar remarks may be found in Dr. WHEWELL's *Novum Organon Re
novatum*, Bk. 2, ch. 5, § 4 ; ch. 6, § 3 ; Bk. 3, ch. 4, § 4.

abstract number is always necessary as "Multiplier." Everywhere the subjective faculty of Introspection or Imagination must reinforce the objective faculty of Perception or outward Observation, or Science must stagnate, Conversation become purposeless and vapid, and Education futile.

Incentives to aspiration.   Although the pursuit of objects or economy of materials will doubtless ever be the more successful when subordinated to the culture of motives, by as much as the known appearance falls short of the unknown reality, yet the contemplation of prospective privileges and distant glories is an important aid to aspiration, especially when our imperfect vision may be assisted by the descriptions and suggestions of more experienced and far-sighted explorers of truth. To a want of faith in our divinely bestowed,—or at least, reverently and thankfully be it spoken, to our divinely purchased and practically possible,—capacity, ever increasingly to comprehend the secrets of the universe without us and within us, we may attribute that general superficiality of the social instinct which constrains mankind to court misery in crowds, while the riches of nature rot in her ample and luxuriant wildernesses. Ignorance makes us miserable, and misery, while loving company, naturally measures that chief blessing rather by the quantity than by the quality, seeking to satisfy in the attainable extent and diversity, its cravings for the too unattainable intensity and geniality. Hence, as has been well observed, while older countries are "groaning under the necessity of contributing to the support of an excessive population," the progress of settlement and civilization "amidst virgin lands, forests and waters, is of an almost geological slowness."* Let us not conclude the consideration of our world-embracing theme without adverting to the anticipations of that eminent patriarch of Science, Sir JOHN HERSCHEL, of the results we may hope to realize when the individual discipline of mind and the general freedom of com-

* "Primeval Forests of the Amazons," *N. Monthly Mag.* vol. 128; LITTELL'S *Living Age*, vol. 78.

munion shall make Conversation truly profitable and Education truly familiar.

" There is something in the contemplation of general laws which powerfully persuades us to merge individual feeling, and to commit ourselves unreservedly to their disposal ; while the observation of the calm, energetic regularity of nature, the immense scale of her operations, and the certainty with which her ends are attained" (*i. e.*, the perception of established order, as the wary writer might perhaps have expressed himself had he not written before the dangers of Pantheism were so distinctly manifested as now) " tends irresistibly to tranquilize and reassure the mind and render it less susceptible to repining, selfish and turbulent emotions. And this it does, not by debasing our nature into weak compliances and abject submission to circumstances, but by filling us, as from an inward spring, with a sense of nobleness and power which enables us to rise superior to them by showing us our strength and innate" (potential) "dignity, and by calling upon us for the exercise of those powers and faculties by which we are susceptible of the comprehension of so much greatness, and which form, as it were, a link between ourselves and the best and noblest benefactors of our species, with whom we hold communion in thoughts, and participate in discoveries which have raised them above the level of their fellow-mortals, and brought them nearer to their Creator."—*Discourse on the Study of Natural Philosophy*, 1831.

" That Astronomers should congregate to talk of stars and planets ; Chemists, of atoms ; Geologists, of strata, is natural enough. But what is there of *equal* mutual interest, *equally* connected with and *equally* pervading all they are engaged upon, which causes their hearts to burn within them for mutual communication and unbosoming? Surely, were each of us to give utterance to all he feels, we would hear the Chemist, the Astronomer, the Physiologist, the Electrician, the Botanist, the Geologist, all with one accord, and each in the language of his own science, declaring not only the wonderful works of GOD disclosed by it, but the delight which their disclosure affords him, and the privilege he feels it to be to have aided in it.   This is indeed a magnificent induction, a consilience* there is no refuting.   It leads us to look onward through the long vista of time, with chastened but confident assurance that Science has still other and nobler work to do than any she has yet attempted ; work which, before she is prepared to attempt, the minds of men must be prepared to receive the attempt—prepared, I mean, by an entire conviction of the wisdom of her views, the purity of her objects, and the faithfulness of her disciples."—*Address to the British Association for the Advancement of Science*, 1845.

Equally hopeful are the utterances of less famous voices of our Western world.   One † of these may perhaps here suffice.

" The highest Science must eventually exhibit a unity which shall correspond with that of Reality.   Indications are not entirely wanting of an approaching re-union between the two great branches of Investigation—those which concern respectively the Material and the Spiritual domains of nature. Our present arbitrary division necessitates a one-sided development of the scientific faculties of the mind.   Physical and Metaphysical study being each vitally connected with the *whole* of Science, it is only by the simultaneous pursuit of *both*, that the inquirer can fit himself for either. . . . . The recognition which is to come of the omnipotence of Love and Thought on the one hand, and of the undeveloped capabilities of the lowest human being on the other, will be accompanied I think, whether as cause or as effect, by a new

* " The Consilience of Inductions takes place when an induction obtained from one class of facts coincides with an induction obtained from another different class. . . . The Consilience of our inductions gives rise to a constant convergence of our Theory towards Simplicity and Unity. . . . That rules springing from remote and unconnected quarters should leap to the same point, can only arise from that being the point where truth resides."—WHEWELL, *Nov. Org. Ren.*, B. 2, ch. 5.

† The author's much lamented friend and kinsman, the late PHILIP PHYSICK RANDOLPH.—1869.

era of Science, Philosophy, Philanthropy and Religion. In their present condition, Science denies the existence of a spiritual world; Philosophy merely affirms the existence of that world; Philanthropy is without a scientific basis for her effort, and Faith is blind to her own power. In the future which we anticipate, the Man of Science will recognize the continent of permanent Fact and invariable Law which is the fairest portion of his domain; the Philosopher will pass beyond the mere recognition of that region, and carry into its exploration the patience and humility which his compeer has displayed in a lower field; the Philanthropist will commence his labor for Man in the study of the Science of Man; and the Believer will gather the full import of the good tidings which are his all in all."

Courteous and patient reader! let the depth   Deprecatory and of this borrowed introspection, and the large-   hortatory. ness of this borrowed aspiration, account for the discursive and partial manner in which only we have been able to deal with so large a subject, and avail to palliate any occasional irregularity in the flow of expression where the continuity of meaning may upon examination be found unbroken. Let us be content with bearing all timely witness, and lending all possible aid, to the progressive transmutation of our human and too discordant Polytechny into a divine and perfectly harmonious Monotechny; and let us part in the faith that all the truths of Science, Conversation and Education are among the "all things" of which the zealous but practical Apostle writes as "pertaining to life and godliness," and so qualify all that has been here said either at first or at second hand respecting them, by the confession that if indeed ours, they can only be so, as the same inspired penman further writes, (when rightly read) "of his Divine power which is given unto us through the knowledge of Him that hath called us by glory and virtue."—2 PET. I, 3.

1868.

AN ASPIRATION.

" Let us go on to perfection."—HEB. vi. 1.

GOAL of devotion, and Spring of affection!
  Quiet our terror, and quicken our hope :—
Rise like a sun for our light and direction :—
  Banish the darkness wherein we yet grope!

Palpable darkness still hovers around us,
  Braving the brightness of thy blessed strength;
Come in thy fullness before it confound us,
  Shine on our effort, and save us, at length!

Voices behind us, and pitfalls before us,
  Hide in the clouds which dispute thy design.
Break their besetments, and richly restore us,
  Ere their contagion our faith undermine.

Where is our standard if Thou shalt forsake us?
  How shall we rally without a device?
What can devices of men but unmake us,
  Ordered themselves as by falling of dice?

Chance-born, if ever chance lives in thy system,
  Diverse and fleeting as hues of the morn,   .
How can they lure their observers to wisdom,
  Past the brief twilight they rose to adorn?

Not as strange gods shall thy sons climb to glory,
  Parted in empire, or hostile in aim :
One in their nature, and one in their story,
  One Love shall bind them, an infinite same.

Rise for the seed of thy holy election!
  Scatter the desperate spirits of ill!
GOD of the just! for thy name is Perfection,
  Gather thine own to repose in thy will!

www.ingramcontent.com/pod-product-compliance
Lightning Source LLC
Chambersburg PA
CBHW030544270326
41927CB00008B/1510